Hope Will Find You

Hope Will Find You

*My Search for the Wisdom to
Stop Waiting and Start Living*

Naomi Levy

HARMONY BOOKS

New York

Harmony Books is a registered trademark and the
Harmony Books colophon is a trademark of
Random House, Inc.

Library of Congress Cataloging-in-Publication Data

Levy, Naomi.

Hope will find you : my search for the wisdom to stop waiting and start living /
Naomi Levy.—1st ed.

p. cm.

1. Consolation (Judaism) 2. Faith (Judaism) 3. God (Judaism) 4. Spiritual
life—Judaism. 5. Hope—Religious aspects—Judaism. 6. Suffering—Religious
aspects—Judaism. 7. Levy, Naomi. 8. Ataxia-telangiectasia in children. I. Title.

BM729.C6L467 2010

296.7—dc22   2010014593

ISBN 978-0-385-53170-2

Printed in the United States of America

Design by Leonard W. Henderson

10 9 8 7 6 5 4 3 2 1

First Edition

For Rob, Adi, and Noa

contents

preface

A book without a preface is like a body without a soul.
RABBINIC PROVERB

When I was a child, my father used to read me bedtime stories from a children's Bible. I couldn't get enough of them. I loved hearing about Eden and the Flood, about Joseph the Dreamer and Moses the Prophet who found God in a withered bush. Every night before turning out the lights, my father would slide his glasses down the bridge of his nose, peer over his frames at me, and ask, "So, Nomi, what's the moral of the story?" I knew my father wanted to teach me to look for lessons, not miracles. I would think for a while until suddenly I could see the point of the story. Then my father would kiss my forehead and turn out the light, and I went to sleep believing in a life that made sense and in a God with a flowing white beard (that's how the book's illustrator drew God) who was in control of it all. Of course, as I grew I learned that life doesn't always make sense. And God? In time I learned to see beyond the beard.

When I grew up and became a rabbi, those bedtime talks with my dad would return to me. I saw I could help people through times of confusion. By far the most common human condition I learned to guide people through is this: an overwhelming feeling that life hasn't yet begun. Throughout my years as a rabbi I counseled so many people waiting for life to begin. They would say to me, "My life will begin when . . ." The people were all different, but the yearning was the same. Life would begin when certain pieces fell into place: *when I lose weight, when I fall in love, when I get a job, when I get married, when I have a baby, when I buy a home, when I get divorced, when I quit my job . . .*

People came to me with their questions: *Rabbi, how do you learn to embrace the present when you don't have what you yearn for? How long do you wait for things to change? How do you find the courage to make a change? What do you do in the meantime? What do you do when you are aware of a yearning but you can't even define what it is that you want or what it is that's missing? What do you do when you have to make a decision and you don't know which way to turn?* And I would listen and offer guidance and hope.

But one day, without warning, I was faced with my own personal crisis. Now I was the one who was waiting for my life to begin. My professional life, my emotional life, my spiritual life were in a state of turmoil.

It's always easier to be the birthing coach than it is to be the one in labor. It's so much easier to hold on to hope for others than it is to believe the answer is coming when you just can't see it coming.

As I struggled with my fear and confusion, I could hear my father lovingly asking me, "So, Nomi, what's the moral of the story?" I was knocked off track—was there any meaning in my holding pattern? The story only begins when you do something, when you courageously take the steps to overcome your fears and boldly set out on a new path. But then I remembered that my father wanted to teach me to look for lessons, not miracles. I thought and thought until suddenly I could see the point of the story. I could see my own life as a journey, as a narrative with an arc that all people must pass through in their own way.

So I offer my story. This book traces a seven-year journey. The crisis I faced, my struggle to embrace the situation I'd been handed, the lessons I learned, and the ways I'm still learning each day to stop waiting on the sidelines and plunge into the action.

One of the most painful aspects of waiting for life to begin is the belief that one's life as it is today has no meaning, isn't interesting enough or powerful enough to be a "real" life. No one wants to live a pointless existence. The reality is, every life just as it is right now has its own unique power and lesson to teach. No life is a chaotic mess devoid of meaning or structure or a message. Every day has its story. Every dream holds a lesson.

There are millions of people who share our struggles. Who isn't longing for something? Who hasn't suffered? Who hasn't gotten stuck or confused or lost? Who hasn't taken a wrong turn? Who isn't frightened?

The moment when we can see how our own story is both a unique *and* a shared experience, that is when we can see how we are no longer alone. That is the moment when we can see our life as a meaningful story that is shared by all people.

I wish I could say I am fully cured, that I never feel lost or stuck. But that would be a lie. Who said it was going to be easy? And who said any of us will arrive at a true and lasting peace? Perhaps a true and lasting peace is a better description of death than of life. Life is a never-ending struggle. But to give up, to give in to helplessness or resignation or paralysis, is to die when we are still alive. And who wants to do that?

The rabbi in me would like to offer a prayer for you. I pray you will learn to see your life as a meaningful story. I pray you will learn to listen to your soul's insistent yearnings. I pray you will come to see just how strong and powerful you are. I pray you will learn to believe you can transform your life. I pray you will learn to live and shine inside your imperfect life and find meaning and joy right where you are.

Most of all I pray you will uncover a great miracle: your extra-ordinary life.

A Blessing

May God bless you and protect you.

May God bless you with wisdom and vision.

May you dream great dreams and may you see them come true.

May you be blessed with courage and the power to be bold.

May you be blessed with kindness, compassion, and hope.

May you be blessed with love, and a loving, resilient heart.

May your smile be contagious, your joy outrageous.

May you shine and light up the world.

Amen.

I Will Fix Her

O N e

One doesn't know another's sorrow.
Yiddish proverb

In January 1999 I received a call from a woman named Pam Smith. Pam told me about her twenty-year-old daughter, Rebecca, who was suffering from a fatal degenerative neurological disease. Pam phoned to ask if I would be willing to be the keynote speaker at an A T fund-raiser she was hosting. I had never heard of the disease. Pam told me ataxia-telangiectasia is a very rare disease affecting only three Caucasian children in a million. Pam said she was inspired by a book I had written.

In 1999 I spent my days writing, delivering lectures around the country, teaching spiritual counseling at a local rabbinical seminary, and together with my husband, Rob, raising our two children, Adi, who was five, and Noa, who was three. I had been a congregational rabbi for seven years, but I chose to leave the congregation so that I could have more-flexible hours for writing, for teaching, and for mothering. When I got Pam's call I was feverishly at work on a new book of prayers, and life was good. I had a wonderful husband and two healthy children.

Of course, I agreed to speak at the A-T fund-raiser, and Pam and I set a time for us all to get together for lunch at a local restaurant. I had no idea what to expect. I didn't know what a young woman with A-T would look like. On the appointed afternoon a van pulled up in front of the restaurant and Rebecca's father, George, wheeled her up to the table beside me. She was quite beautiful, with straight shiny dark brown hair, ivory skin, and a glowing smile. When I asked Rebecca about school it was hard to understand what she was saying because her speech was so slurred. I could tell she was getting frustrated because I kept turning to her parents for a translation. Her body had been ravaged by this cruel disease. I could see Rebecca was angry. She was angry to have to be so dependent upon her parents at an age when she needed to rebel and carve out her own identity. All her friends were driving, were at college, were dancing at parties. And she was fighting for life. The pain in her parents' faces was palpable. Pam said to me, "I don't have bad days. Every day with Rebecca is a good day." Yes, Rebecca was a gift. And I'm certain Pam treasured every moment with her. And I could see the sadness behind Pam's smile. Why should such a blessed child have to suffer so?

Rebecca's father, George, ran a very successful real-estate financing company. He was a self-made man who was used to getting what he wanted. The tragedy was, he had made enough money to give Rebecca anything her heart desired, but this man who was larger than life was helpless to cure his child. There was no cure for A-T. No treatment. A diagnosis of A-T was a certain death sentence. Period. George and Pam's response to all their feelings of helplessness was to create a foundation to raise money for A-T research. Through their foundation they had already raised millions. Yet there was no cure or treatment in sight.

I couldn't begin to imagine the torment Rebecca and her parents were living with daily. And the hope. Rebecca was considered something of a miracle in the world of A-T. Most kids with A-T don't make it out of their teens.

On the day of the fund-raiser there must have been seven hundred people gathered together in support of Rebecca and her family. Every speaker talked about hope for finding a cure. They showed a video about Rebecca. I saw her walking around happily as a toddler and then we all watched scenes of her gradual decline, scenes of her bravery and her struggles for life. We watched her riding her horse with such joy. Then I got up and spoke about Rebecca's courage and her family's dedication to finding a cure for this horrible disease. That very week was Rebecca's twenty-first birthday and Pam asked me to bless her. Rebecca slowly came up on stage all by herself with crutches. There was such determination and joy that shone through her eyes. I closed my eyes, put my hands on her head, and blessed her with a birthday blessing. I prayed for Rebecca's health, for her strength; I prayed for a cure. I could hear the weeping in the room.

What did I believe? Did I believe in a God who could cure Rebecca? Did I believe God would miraculously undo what nature and genes had done? No. Not exactly. But I wanted to believe it. I remembered listening once to a preacher on the radio who said, "If God says you can catch a whale, then start cracking out the tartar sauce!" I prayed for that kind of faith in God's supernatural powers and at the same time I prayed for Rebecca's doctors. I hoped scientists could learn to correct the problem, treat the problem, cure the problem.

A scientist named Dr. Becket then took the stage to receive an award for his incredible breakthroughs in A-T research. He played a movie about his lab and the amazing advances he was making with the help of Rebecca's family. He said there was a blessing in Rebecca having A-T because her illness had led to the funding of such important research. I gasped when he spoke those words. As far as I was concerned, there was nothing good about Rebecca's A-T. No blessing in it.

I felt so sorry for Rebecca and her family. And yes, I felt so blessed and relieved that my own children were perfectly healthy.

I came home that day from the fund-raiser and wrapped my arms around both my kids and squeezed them with so much gratitude for all our blessings.

Two years passed. It was July 2001.

t w o

God gave burdens, also shoulders.
YIDDISH PROVERB

M Y JOURNEY began innocently enough.

The phone was ringing. It was Friday night, the Sabbath, and our home was full of guests and great food and kids and blessings. My mom was visiting from Boston. Normally I would have ignored the ringing. But without thinking, I got up, my legs walked me into the kitchen, my arm extended, my hand put the receiver against my ear.

"Hello?"

"Rabbi Levy?"

"Yes."

"This is Dr. Becket." Yes, the same doctor who had received an award at Rebecca's fund-raiser. "I have the results of your daughter's blood test."

There was an excited bounce in his voice. I was relieved. I just knew it would be negative—*Noa's fine, she's healthy, she's* . . . My legs carried me to my bedroom; I closed the door behind me.

"I had a suspicion I was right about her," I heard the doctor say. "The test took months. Her cells just wouldn't grow. She's got A-T. She does."

That same joyful bounce in his voice. And yet this man had just told me that my daughter, my Noa, my baby, my five-year-old angel with long golden curls and big brown puddle eyes, sitting in the dining room right then in a pink dress with fairy wings she refused to ever take off, had a fatal degenerative disease, the same one that had afflicted Rebecca Smith.

My legs crumbled beneath me. I was sitting on the floor. I started squeaking. Crying.

"Most parents are so grateful when I give them the news," he said to me.

"Grateful? They're GRATEFUL?" I hung up. I hung up on my daughter's doctor.

I couldn't move. It was Friday night, the Sabbath, I had a home full of guests, a table set with roast chicken, fried onions, roasted potatoes. And so many blessings. My mom was in town. Oy, that woman had already suffered enough. She had watched a man shoot my father. She had watched her love get shot right in front of her. She could still see it in her dreams. Sometimes with her eyes wide open. I was pinned to the floor by a gravitational force so strong I felt like the wood beneath me was about to give way and I would be sucked into the center of hell itself.

I could hear the laughter in the dining room. A Hollywood producer we'd invited, it turned out, grew up just blocks from my home in Brooklyn. He and my mom were engrossed in a conversation about the old neighborhood. The kids were running around the living room with drums and spoons. My husband, Rob, was

8

clearing the dishes. I heard the sink running, a knife scraping against a plate.

I'd been missing for quite some time. I felt sad for Rob. He was whistling and filling the dishwasher. I wished he wouldn't ever open the bedroom door. Right then he walked in and found me on the floor. He got down on his knees; I must have looked like hell. I shared the news. Now both of us were stuck to the floor. We had a house full of guests. My mom was reminiscing with the Hollywood producer. Noa was running around the living room with her fairy wings. We couldn't move.

I had no idea how much time passed. My mom walked into our bedroom. She was seventy-eight, with terrible asthma. I was afraid to tell her the news. But how could I keep it from her when she found us both plastered to the floor? I told her in a staccato of gasps and wails. My mom wasn't getting sucked down into the floor. My mom was so strong. She was standing on her feet. She took my hand and I came unglued from the floor. We were all lying on my bed. She's a little Jewish bubby, a grandmother, from Poland, but Ruth Levy is tough. She hypnotized me with words of comfort and second opinions. She said, "How can a doctor who calls with bad results during Shabbat dinner possibly know anything?"

Our guests let themselves out. I crawled into bed with Noa, trying to match my breaths to hers; her deep sleep sighs were my lullaby. I could feel the warmth of her little body zipped inside her footsie pj's. I spent the night tethered to her.

In the morning Noa yawned, stretched, and squealed with excitement to find me curled up next to her in bed. *Such a morning person, my Noa.*

"Mommy, what are you doing here?"

"I missed you" is the truth that poured out of me with a forced smile.

Adi, my seven-year-old son, came bounding down the ladder of the bunk bed they shared and jumped on us both. That morning he was so eager with anticipation he could barely contain himself. The next day was his birthday. That's why my mom was in from Boston. We were having a party for him with eighteen of his classmates. I was trying so hard to hold myself together as we were snuggling on Noa's lower bunk, but I thought I might burst.

I ran to my bedroom, shut the door, and crawled into bed. Rob was already up. He'd been up for hours—scooping dog poop, setting up tables, getting the yard ready for the next day's festivities. Rob seemed to be handling this so much better than I was. He was moving, I was sinking.

If you had observed the two of us on this one morning, you could already make out the divergent contours of a singular anguish that would overtake two frightened, suffering parents over the next several years. He did, I watched. He achieved, I stared. He worked, paid the bills, cooked dinner every night, and even managed to find time to play tennis and walk the dog; I sat.

I knew this land I was traveling to. I had lived there before, when my father was murdered. Who can forget such a land? I knew every inch of terrain. I knew its latitude and longitude and its most memorable feature: walls. I had walked it, worked in it, and even set sail from it. But there it was again on the horizon all spread out before me. It's never easy to be a person with two countries. Living here and longing to be there, arriving there and yearning to be here.

Later in the day we phoned Rob's parents to tell them the news about Noa. Like my mother, they offered encouragement. Rob's mom,

Sari, said with confidence, "There's nothing wrong with this child." His dad, Aaron, was equally optimistic. I knew they were shaken, but they were going to help us find the right specialists to see; this must all be some mistake. Rob's dad was on the board of a hospital in LA. He would help us. It was comforting to hear their pragmatic plans, people to see, actions to take.

Then came the party. I was doing this. I was throwing every ounce of my emptied-out soul into this birthday party. I was laughing, running activity centers in cutoff jeans, a purple Lakers sweatshirt, and bare feet.

Our backyard was transformed into Italy. Twenty energetic kids sucked down pasta. Noa asked me to do the "Oh what a night, what a beautiful night" Disney song with a single strand of pasta between us. My heart was breaking; our lips met in a slimy wet kiss. Then all twenty kids took off their shoes and socks, rolled up their pants, and stomped on wine grapes in a giant red tub.

Watching Noa at the grapes, it was apparent why she'd been through so many tests. There was something wrong. Rob and I were trying not to notice. But she didn't walk until she was two, and even at five she teetered like a toddler. She was constantly losing her balance, falling down. She was dizzy and woozy, and spoke with a slur. People sometimes stared and pitied us, but we found ways to lie to ourselves.

She looked so beautiful. And naked without her fairy wings, but she didn't want them to get ruined at the party. It was a fun and original party. Parents came at the end, they hung out with us. One mom took me aside and told me how jealous she was of our lives. Yeah. If she only knew.

Adi was in heaven. His intelligent brown eyes were magnified by his thick round Harry Potter glasses. My son at seven years of age was cute, stubborn, and extremely sensitive. He cried when he saw a homeless mother pushing her baby in a shopping cart and wanted to help. He was extremely tactile, needed lots of hugs, and had a frightening memory.

He knew all the lyrics to *West Side Story*, his favorite movie those days. ("Dear kindly Judge, Your Honor, my parents treat me rough, with all their marijuana they won't give me a puff . . .") He had a fantastic sense of humor and the most contagious laugh.

Adi was stomping grapes near Noa. He loved and hated his little sister and absolutely refused to see that there was anything the matter with her. People were always treating Noa with great caution and care; Adi was constantly grabbing toys out of her hand and pushing her down.

I loved him for this even more than I already loved him. He was the only person in the world who treated Noa like a regular kid. Noa worshipped him.

Later that night Rob grabbed me tight and made the following oath: "If we get to dodge this bullet, we will never complain again." I squeezed him close and made a silent promise to myself: "I will fix Noa. I will give her every therapy under the sun, as God is my witness, I will fix her."

What Happened to You?

t h r e e

When it falls, it falls butter side down.
Yiddish proverb

Fixing Noa was a full-time job. There was preschool in the mornings and then Noa and I set off on her therapeutic regimen. Physical therapy, occupational therapy, speech therapy, swimming therapy, equestrian therapy, vision therapy. I wanted to try everything. I was running us both ragged. Everywhere I took Noa, I met mothers like me in waiting rooms. Mothers who were determined to spend every last cent they had and all their time and energy to "fix" their child.

The days slid by. I stopped working, teaching, writing.

In the late afternoons, after all the therapies, I'd pick Adi up from school. I spent my life in the car. One day after school Adi asked me:

"So, Mom, how many years was college?"

"Four."

"And how many was rabbinical school?"

"Technically, six."

He did some calculating in his head and then:

"All those years, and *now* look at you."

He was referring to my career as a chauffeur.

"Thanks a lot, sweetheart!"

Ouch.

The next day, a cool and sunny Friday morning in November, I got the kids ready for school but didn't exactly have time to get myself ready. I looked tired and disheveled. I was wearing Rob's blue sweatshirt with my hair pulled back in one of Noa's hair clips. After dropping Adi and Noa off at school, I had coffee with another woman rabbi. She'd been trying to set this coffee date with me for some time, but I'd been having trouble returning phone calls. Finally, she pinned me down. Sipping a latte, she blurted out:

"What happened to you?"

"What do you mean?"

"You used to be a rising star."

OUCH. I was a falling star. I knew what she was referring to. I had been in the first class of women to enter the Conservative rabbinical seminary. I had been the first female Conservative rabbi to head a solo pulpit on the West Coast. I had published a book and was almost done with a second book. *And now look at me.* I had no ambition. None left. I was so tired. I didn't know where I ended and Noa began. If her leg hurt, my leg started hurting. If she felt dizzy, I felt dizzy. I had only one ambition: *I will fix her, as God is my witness, I will fix her.* The rest was a blur.

four

No one knows whose shoe pinches.

"TELL ME about the rabbits, George," I asked Rob as I lay beside him in bed at night. It was a famous line from Steinbeck's *Of Mice and Men*. In the book, Lennie, who is mentally disabled, asks his friend George to paint him a picture of how wonderful life will be when their dreams come true. *Tell me tales of comfort.* I was drowning and Rob seemed to be rising. I wanted him to describe the world as he saw it. The world of hope. Rob refused to believe Noa was sick.

The two of us had completely switched places. When we first married I was working full-time as a congregational rabbi and Rob was freelancing as a journalist out of the house. When Adi was born Rob stayed home and took care of him while I went off to the synagogue each day. He took Adi to the park, shopped, cooked. Now Rob was working full-time at the *Los Angeles Jewish Journal* and I was . . . sinking. It's not that I was sitting idle—I was getting the kids ready for school in the morning, driving carpool, taking Noa to her doctors and therapies, picking up Adi from school, playing with

17

the kids, helping with homework—it's that I just felt lost, that I had lost my direction, my focus, my calling, my buoyancy.

As I was falling, Rob was moving up the ranks of his paper from freelancer to staff writer to managing editor to editor in chief. In his spare time he was feverishly writing a screenplay. He sold the screenplay. And he still found the time every night to shop and cook dinner for our family.

I couldn't understand how Rob was so productive when I was so lost. "Tell me about the rabbits, George." *Paint your world for me.* I knew there was suffering behind Rob's success. Others saw a young father finding his stride; they couldn't see what was chasing him. Rob told me he would be at work and he'd suddenly be seized by fear. Panic about Noa's condition would grip at his chest and send his heart racing until his whole body was covered in sweat, but he would willfully push it out of his mind. Instead he'd focus on one piece of hope. When the fear threatened to overwhelm him, he'd work even harder to avoid thinking about what was going on. "How do you do that?" I asked. "Denial," Rob said, "don't underestimate it."

I didn't know how to throw myself into work; I couldn't concentrate. I was terrible at denial.

As I sat in the waiting rooms, I found comfort in fantasy, in memory, in daydreams.

In the waiting rooms I'd slip into the most vivid daydreams. I was flooded with memories. I'd suddenly come face-to-face with people from my past.

five

If you want your dreams to come true, don't sleep.
YIDDISH PROVERB

ONE DAY in late October as I was sitting in a waiting room watching my life slip away from me, I flashed on a memory of Bo.

I was a congregational rabbi in Venice, California, for seven years. Venice is one of the world's homeless capitals. Homeless people would sleep on the synagogue's porch every night. By morning they'd pack up all their belongings and head off to Venice Beach.

One homeless man was very friendly to me. "Good morning, Rabbi. How are you doing today, Rabbi?" he'd say each day. I could smell the alcohol on his breath. Over time I got to know him.

His name was Bo. His hair was a mess. He was missing his front teeth. His skin was so weathered it was hard to tell how old he was. Bo always smiled and was very polite, and he was always asking me for money. I could never say no to Bo.

One morning Bo approached me, "I have a question, Rabbi." I was sure Bo was asking me for money. I reached into my pocket, but Bo simply said, "I'd like to study with you."

"You'd like to study with me? What would you like to study?"

"The Bible," he sniffed, and scratched himself.

"We'll see."

There were a lot of people I was trying to get to study with me, but getting them to carve out an hour for God was like pulling teeth.

Week after week, "Good morning, Rabbi. Let me hold the door for you, Rabbi. Can we study, Rabbi?"

It turned out that my most eager student was Bo.

Finally I said, "I'm going to buy you all the items you need to get clean. If you come to me clean and completely sober, we can study on Thursday mornings at ten."

I went out to the drugstore and bought toothpaste, a toothbrush, a razor, shaving cream, shampoo, a comb, a bar of soap, a roll of quarters, and laundry detergent.

The next time I saw Bo I handed him a shopping bag full of personal-care items. I reminded him, "Clean clothes, shower, shave, brush—and you have to be sober."

Bo smiled his toothless smile and ran off.

The next Thursday Bo showed up at the temple. His hair was combed. He was clean. He was wearing a button-down shirt he had gotten at the St. Joseph Center and a pair of gray corduroy pants.

We walked into the temple's library. Bo sat down on the brown couch, I sat opposite him.

"What would you like to study?"

"The Book of Jonah," he said.

I took out Bibles and we started reading. Bo was smart. He knew his scripture. Jonah is a book about the Prophet Jonah. God calls out to him to send him on a mission, and he tries to run away from God. He gets on a ship and tries to sail away from God.

Bo was fascinated by Jonah. He wanted to know all about him, what I thought of him.

Week after week Bo showed up clean and sober and we studied and talked. Always about Jonah.

Sometimes Bo didn't show up. When I'd meet him on the street I could tell he'd been drinking. Then the following week he'd be back in the library with me all animated and excited.

I asked him, "Why are you so interested in Jonah?" He said, "'Cause I feel like Jonah." Then he went into his beautiful analysis. He said, "There are two prophets who get the call and face a storm on the sea: Noah and Jonah. Noah gets the call, he listens, and gets to ride out the storm in an ark. Jonah gets the call, tries to run away from God and sinks, and ends up in the belly of a whale. And Rabbi," he said to me, "I'm in the whale."

Bo went on, "I could have had it all: a home, a wife, kids. I could have been a teacher. But I was running away and chasing after other gods. I traded it all in for the drink and the needle."

I said to Bo, "Do you know where Jonah finally found God? Right in the belly of that whale. It's time for you to find God, Bo."

Bo got very excited. He said, "God's with me in the belly of the whale."

Watching Bo, I so wanted to believe he could turn his life around. I wanted to believe that it's never too late to change. I thought about the ways we all run from the call of God or the call of our souls. But Bo's life had spun out too long and too far. Bo began the process of changing his life, but he could never get out of the belly of the whale. He died of AIDS.

Sitting in that waiting room, I saw myself inside Bo's whale. I couldn't figure out how to keep things in perspective. I couldn't figure out how to get my life back on track again. Fighting for Noa's health had become my obsession.

Thinking of Bo, I whispered to myself, *"It's never too late" is a lie.* Suddenly I saw the danger of putting things off, of dropping out of life the way I had. I understood that if you wait for the right moment to appear, it might never come. I told myself: *You're waiting to be saved from above, but transformation requires effort from below. You keep telling yourself you've got plenty of time to get back on track, but time has better things to do than to stick around waiting for you.*

Was God calling me? What was I running from? What was I hiding from? What was I putting off?

Bo waited too long, but even in his final months he found a way to become a great teacher. He taught a rabbi how to read the Bible with new eyes, and how to encounter the homeless with a new reverence.

I was whispering a silent blessing to Bo: *May God be with you in the belly of the whale. May you find peaceful seas.* Suddenly a little girl in the waiting room started shrieking and her cries whisked me back to the present. The girl with red curls and freckles was sitting in her stroller and she'd dropped her security blanket on the floor. I leaned down and handed her the soggy shredded yellow cloth. She grabbed it from me, gave me a hateful glare for having even touched her sacred treasure, and began sucking on it as if it were a bottle or a breast. I gave the little girl's mother a knowing smile.

Noa had been a blanky baby too. As the little redheaded girl settled into her blanky, I settled back into my thoughts. I was smiling, remembering a scene with Noa and her blanky.

SIX

O Lord, I am in straits; You be my security.

ISAIAH 38:14

NOA, GOD bless her, was not an easy baby. She turned colic into an art form. She cried and cried all day and all night. She never slept. We didn't even bother to put her in a crib at night. She'd spend the night in a stroller beside our bed and Rob and I would take turns jiggling her.

Then somehow we found her a red satin blanket that miraculously calmed her. Noa would clutch "red blanky" for dear life. One week we flew to Boston to visit my mom and we lost the red blanket on the airplane. We were sitting in my mother's apartment and Rob and I looked at each other thinking: *She's not going to sleep without red blanky.*

Faced with the prospect of a sleepless night, Rob was on a mission to find Noa a replacement blanky. It was about 6:00 p.m. and he raced through the neighborhood to the baby store. It was closed. He went right and left and all the stores were closing. No blanky in sight.

In the meantime there I was in my mom's apartment desperately trying to put Noa to sleep. Noa was doing her best imitation of Linda

Blair in *The Exorcist*, screaming in a deep raspy voice, "Blanky, blanky!"

Finally Rob showed up at my mother's apartment with a huge, I mean gargantuan, XXX Large pair of red satin lady's underwear that looked like they could fit a hippo. Noa saw them and cheered, "Blanky!" I was laughing so hard tears were rolling down my face as I watched my daughter clutching this huge pair of panties for dear life.

I remembered a parable I once read in a Hasidic commentary by Rabbi Sholom Noach Berezovsky called *Paths of Peace* that said a baby can be playing happily with a useless object, say, a torn sock, and if the mother takes the sock away he'll start crying in bitter anguish as if his whole world has gone black. The mother laughs because she knows the sock is worthless. But to the child the sock is his whole universe. The same is true with us. We let setbacks throw us and God can't believe how narrow our vision is. The things we think are important are of no significance at all—all the material stuff we pine after, our yearnings for success. In God's eyes, it's all socks.

As I sat in that claustrophobic waiting room I asked myself: What kind of underwear was I clutching? Maybe Noa's condition had become my security blanket. Maybe I was using it as an excuse to drop out of life. What was God thinking of me and my narrow vision? What did God want from me? I knew parents who had kids with special needs who were unstoppable. Taking care of their kids and holding down jobs and juggling it all with such grace. I thought of Rebecca's parents, who started a foundation for A-T research. What should I be doing with my days? What more could I be doing?

Should. Could. So much judgment. I had so little compassion for this frightened mother.

Just then the waiting-room door opened and Noa emerged from

her physical therapy session all wobbly and full of smiles. She took my hand and it felt so good to hold on to her. Just touching her soft skin grounded me, brought me back into this life and lifted me, at least for this one magical moment, out of my thoughts and memories and worries.

There is something unusually calming about Noa. Rob would take her out for lunch and come home and tell me, "I just spent the afternoon with my Zen master." Noa wore little gold wire-rimmed eyeglasses and occasionally she'd slide them down the bridge of her nose and glance at me over them, and suddenly the tables would turn between us. She was the all-knowing parent taking me in with wisdom and love. The look she'd give me was the exact look my father used to give me when he'd gaze at me lovingly over his glasses.

What did my child know that I didn't know?

I was lost in a world of doctors and therapies and insurance companies. How could I return to my rabbinic calling? Where did God fit into this picture? How come I couldn't feel God? Where was God?

Months passed.

I could feel anger beginning to bubble up inside me.

seven

Don't spit in the well, you might drink from it later.
YIDDISH PROVERB

ONE MORNING after dropping the kids off at school, I was shopping for groceries and I bumped into one of my former congregants in the cereal aisle. Her name was Alice, and she was in her seventies. She looked at me and said, "Rabbi, you look haggard, absolutely haggard."

I hate my life, I whispered to myself as I walked away from her. I hate my life. That's certainly a refrain I came to know well. There was so much to be hateful for. It broke my heart to see my daughter struggle to gain skills that came so easily to other children. I was tired of fighting with the insurance company and the school district for services that Noa so clearly needed. (During assessments I became a reverse stage mother. I'd hope for Noa to fail her "auditions" miserably so that she could get the funding she deserved.) I was tired of waiting in waiting rooms. I was tired of the moms who pitied me. I was tired of worrying, tired of the uncertainty of it all. I was frustrated with my own reaction to the situation I was in. I would flash on Pam Smith, Rebecca's mother, and how she'd smiled and told me, "I don't have bad days." I was having lots of bad days. Why wasn't I heroic like Rebecca's parents? Why wasn't I taking it all in stride? Why wasn't I facing this trial with equanimity and serenity?

Rob's parents were the most active, optimistic people I knew. Up at the crack of dawn, exercising on the beach, involved in all sorts of charities and boards. Rob's dad was a stockbroker who loved his profession and would never retire. The two of them went out almost every night of the week. His mom at seventy-three tap-danced twice a week, volunteered at a hospital, and still wore a bikini to the beach and looked amazing in it. His dad went by the nickname Bunny and it fit him perfectly. He was ever cheerful, ever ready. We had to move in with Sari and Bunny for a month when our house was being repaired due to water damage. I couldn't get over their pace and their spirit. Friends of mine who knew my in-laws would say, "I hope I have their energy when I get to be that age." But I wanted their attitude now.

I was angry. I felt abandoned by God.

eight

*Save me, O God; for the waters have
come up to my soul.*
PSALM 69:2

I BROUGHT the kids home from school one day after we'd moved
back in and our dog, Sophie, was missing. This wasn't exactly a surprise; Sophie was the dog from hell. An adorable nine-year-old beagle
who was part Houdini, part Satan. She was constantly grabbing food
out of the kids' hands, constantly jumping on Noa and knocking her
over to steal a cookie from her. She chewed our blinds, ate our shoes,
tore apart the garbage under our sink. Rob loved this animal. I kept
hoping she'd escape and find a new family to terrorize. But somehow
Sophie was a boomerang; she always found her way back. About once
a week there was a message on our answering machine saying, "I've
got your dog." Inevitably people would tell me how they'd risked
their lives running into oncoming traffic to whisk Sophie out of this
or that boulevard.

I left the kids with a neighbor and went driving around calling out
Sophie's name. Eventually, I found Sophie in an alley rolling in some
homeless person's diarrhea. I wrapped her in newspaper, dragged her

into my car, rolled down the windows, made my way home, picked up the kids from my neighbor, dumped Sophie into Adi's bathtub, and began sobbing as I scrubbed her down. Normally, Sophie was just a nuisance. These days she was dragging me over the edge.

I thought about Bo some more. Bo had gotten so excited when I told him Jonah found God right in the belly of the whale. He believed me. But now I was drowning and where was God? What happened to my solid faith? How come I couldn't find God in my whale?

The question made me think of Bernard.

When I was in college I was a counselor at a summer camp. We were about to take a canoe trip with thirty 10-year-old kids. There were three of us counselors, and as we were preparing for this trip I asked, "Is there anything we need to know?" I'm not a great swimmer and I had zero experience in the canoe department. "No, don't worry, Bernard will be with you," I was told, "and you'll all have life jackets."

Bernard was on the camp's tripping staff and he was exceptionally bright. This was the summer of the Rubik's Cube. Every kid was walking around the sports field twisting a Rubik's Cube. Bernard would take the cube out of their hands, make a couple of twists, and in fifteen seconds it was done. You could time him.

We set out on our canoe trip on an overcast Sunday morning. This wasn't a trip on some lazy river, but in huge open waters. We sat three in a canoe except for Bernard, who was all alone in his. We packed the canoes with sleeping bags, backpacks, food, and gear.

Everything was going fine, the kids were singing. One smart aleck named Shawn was mouthing off and refusing to paddle, but Shawn was always mouthing off. Shawn was the cool kid I wanted to strangle all summer long. He always wore a black T-shirt with the sleeves rolled up and black jeans.

Suddenly the weather started to turn bad. It was gray and the waves were really picking up and we were in the middle of nowhere with the shore a long distance away.

Soon the waves got so high that they were dumping water into our canoes. In a flash, one of the canoes started sinking. It was surreal to watch these kids sinking into the water.

When you see someone sinking, your immediate response is to grab them into your canoe. But the canoes that took in the sinking kids started sinking too.

Then that cool kid, Shawn, the pain-in-the-neck kid, went into some sort of shock. His whole body stiffened up. We lifted him into our canoe and had to lay him facedown across the bottom of the canoe. He wouldn't bend.

Now our canoe started going down. It was pandemonium: waves, kids screaming, and Shawn—who had turned into a human surfboard. All our belongings, our sleeping bags and clothing, everything was at the bottom of the sea.

All of a sudden we saw Bernard paddling up to the right of us. "Bernard!" I yelled. He was paddling away from us. The kids saw him and screamed, "Bernard! Bernard!" He was canoeing away from us. He was paddling so hard and fast that the tip of his canoe was actually out of the water. And soon, like lightning, he was nothing but a dot on the horizon.

Some of us cheered Bernard on as he paddled past us, assuming he was rushing ahead to call for help. But all our generosity of spirit was wasted on Bernard. He paddled himself all the way to a distant shore to wait out the storm by himself while the rest of us were bobbing in the waves screaming for help.

*   *   *

As I tried to make sense of the fate of my innocent child I asked myself, Was God on some distant shore?

My life was falling back on itself. In the span of six short months I had somehow gotten trapped in Bo's whale with Bernard for a God.

A Seven-Year Wait

NINe

It's good to have hope, it's the waiting that spoils it.

YIDDISH PROVERB

Rob's parents made good on their promise. His dad was able to get Noa appointments with the best minds in LA. She saw geneticists and neurologists and teams of doctors who worked up her case in tandem.

Now it was a night like all others: Rob was cooking an amazing Italian dinner, Adi was writing a story for school about a pirate, Noa was fighting off Sophie. Just then my sister, Mimi, called me. It was January 2002. Noa's doctors conferred with one another. They had each put Noa through batteries of tests. They prodded Noa, poked her, measured every square inch of her body, even her earlobes. There were heated phone calls back and forth. They chastised Dr. Becket (the one I hung up on) for calling me directly at home without first consulting them. Mimi, who is a doctor, became the clearing station. That night she presented me with the news, "Nomi, Noa's doctors are saying there's a chance Noa might not have a degenerative disease. They're not sure what she has. It might take years for

35

things to become clear." Mimi was trying to paint me a tiny window of hope.

My dear friend Helene, who is also a doctor, was comforting me. She said this was encouraging news. Nothing was a certainty, nothing was sealed. I was so trying to climb into Mimi's tiny window.

There were more tests we could take, but I didn't want to put Noa through them for an ailment that had no known cure, nor did I trust that the test results would be 100 percent accurate.

Both Mimi and Helene explained the situation to me: only time would tell. Noa was almost six. By the time she was thirteen she would either get progressively stronger or progressively weaker. We would have to wait it out.

Waiting. It had overtaken my life. I spent my days in the waiting rooms of Noa's therapy sessions. I waited behind a two-way mirror.

I kept looking for signs that I would be able to keep her. I kept looking, but I couldn't see.

I prayed to God, but I got no answer. When I thought of God, I'd flash on Bernard and his canoe. I thought God was my help, but God was letting me drown. I was screaming, "Help!" And God was paddling away.

One morning in February just a week before her sixth birthday, Noa told me her dream:

"I had a date with God last night," she said. "God was the most beautiful princess and God and me had dinner at a restaurant and then we were sitting in the car talking and Daddy came up to the car and God had to hide because she didn't want Daddy to see her." As

I listened, I feared the dream was a signal that God was preparing to take my child from me.

That night I gave God a piece of my mind. "You stay away from my baby. Just stay away from her. She's mine and you can't have her. I mean it. You don't know who you're messing with."

You should have seen how I was shaking.

ten

Suspense is worse than the ordeal itself.

YIDDISH PROVERB

IT WAS Noa's sixth birthday. How could it not be a bittersweet occasion? She was so excited my heart was aching. Seven girls were stringing beads and running around our backyard. There was plenty to be thankful for. Noa was doing a bit better, she was making small strides in her therapies. She was showing no signs of degeneration or decline. And yet it was painful to watch her beside her peers. They were light-years ahead of her, swinging across the monkey bars, hanging upside down.

I had spent half the night baking and decorating a Barbie doll cake for Noa. I stripped one of her Barbies, baked a cake in the shape of a hoop skirt, shoved the doll into the skirt, and iced the naked doll and her cake skirt to look like a fairy princess in the most exquisite gown. I put six candles on her cake, plus one for good luck, of course. Was it silly to believe in such a thing as good luck? What did this new birthday year have in store for Noa? I cautioned myself, *Don't look forward, look here.*

I brought out the cake and Noa was in ecstasy. Rob snapped photos, lit the candles. We sang the "Happy Birthday" song to her; she closed her eyes, made a wish, and blew. We clapped, I cried. Rob and I locked eyes across the picnic table. He held me in his eyes with such love and hurt.

"What'd you wish for?" one girl asked Noa. Another butted in, "Don't tell or it won't come true." *Don't tell, Noa, for heaven's sake don't tell.*

e L e v e N

Man plans and God laughs.

YIDDISH PROVERB

THE YEAR 2002 slipped by, one month melting into another.

Occasionally I would replay Noa's dream in my mind. Perhaps Noa's dream represented a possible sign of hope. But I was too lost and blind to see that. Noa saw God as the most beautiful princess. I saw a body snatcher.

After all, God had snatched my father from me when I was a kid.

I could picture the scene like it was yesterday.

It was a beautiful day in June; I was fifteen. My mother removed my father's top drawer from its dresser. It was lying across the bed my parents shared, like an open wooden casket. The next day my father was being buried. People were pressing my mother for answers she did not know. "Did he have life insurance?" "Did he have a safe-deposit box?" "You must find the key." The police were there all morning with six massive black binders full of mug shots. "Do you recognize him?" "Was this the shooter?" They were pressing her. "Mrs. Levy, look carefully." My mother didn't know. She couldn't think. She couldn't see the man's face in her flashbacks. She had been walking down the street with my father at night when a mugger came out of nowhere, pointed a gun at them, asked for their money, then panicked when my father reached for his wallet and shot him. Through her tears the photos were a blur. The police left. My mother collapsed onto the bed she used to share with my father. My father's drawer was beside her.

It was his private drawer, where he kept his secret stuff. I'd always been a snoop and regularly rummaged through my parents' drawers. I played dress-up in my mother's slips and stockings. I messed with her makeup, put on her bright red lipstick and powdered my nose with her Revlon compact. But I had never breached my father's top drawer. I instinctively knew not to go there. The drawer had an aura about it that seemed to say, *Keep out*. And there it was, all exposed and unprotected.

How can I describe my father? He was as good and kind and decent as a person can be. He loved deeply and generously. My father wasn't shy, but he was a man of few words, the opposite of a schmoozer. Although he stood at only five foot three, he had a presence that could light up a room, especially when he was singing. He loved music, and had a beautiful singing voice. He loved studying biblical texts and going to synagogue and watching baseball games. He was a devoted and doting father and a passionate and loving husband.

I can tell you my parents' marriage was a love affair. Everyone could see that. When he first started dating my mother, my grandparents weren't crazy about my dad because he didn't have a lot of money. They wanted my mother to marry a wealthy dentist, but my mother defied them and married the man who gave her love.

My parents had four kids together and lived a fairy-tale existence, except that my dad didn't love his work. He enlisted in the army during World War II and when he came home he never found the time to finish college. Instead, he inherited his father's small clothing manufacturing business, which never nourished his soul or his pockets.

Because of his quiet nature, I learned to read my father's face. I'd follow him around the house like a duckling. I'd watch him in the mornings as he packed lunch and got ready for work. I could see he was bracing himself to face another long day at the shop. When he came home, I watched how he closed his eyes and held my mother in his arms. I could see how deeply their souls were intertwined.

I watched his face light up when he was talking about the subjects that excited him. My dad dreamed of going back and finishing college.

But there was still plenty of time for that, wasn't there?

My mother reached her hand into the drawer and pulled out mementos from my father's days in the army. There was an army ID card. There were Chinese coins my father had brought back from his tour of duty. I remember him telling me the locals liked to call him "Little Buddha" because, like the Buddha, he had a round belly and a contagious, angelic smile. My mother dug further and found stock certificates. They were worthless. Certificates for stocks in companies that were defunct. There was a leather notepad with a gold pen attached. She pulled out a fountain pen as well. There was a gold Timex watch, the kind with the row of metal teeth that expand over your wrist. There were old tortoiseshell glasses in there. And the clip-on sunglasses for my father's Clark Kent frames. I wondered where my father's glasses were. What did they do with them when he died? He never took off his glasses; he couldn't see a thing without them. Whenever I saw him without glasses he looked positively naked.

My mother pulled out several sheets of folded lined paper. It was a eulogy my father had written for his friend Al. In the eulogy my father was trying to make sense of Al's untimely death. He was trying to make sense of a life cut short. I wished he knew then how little time *he* had left. Maybe he would have taken more risks. Maybe he would have gone back to school and finished college like he was always promising to do. Maybe he would have taken a vacation with my mother.

My mother emptied out the entire drawer. I could see the flat wooden bottom of my father's private drawer. There were tiny slips of paper strewn about. Were they grocery receipts? Suddenly I heard a loud wailing coming out of my mother. A moaning full of such deep sadness. They were lottery tickets. She could see now that my father was hoping to be released from his dead-end work. Suddenly the full measure of my father's tragic death took shape before my eyes. My dad was a secret dreamer. And now my dad and his dreams and all the years he thought he had left would make their way into God's private drawer. Why did God let my dad die so young in such a tragic way? That's part of God's secret stuff, and I instinctively knew not to go there.

At the age of fifteen, those lottery tickets became a symbol to me. I imagined my dad was waiting for a miracle. If he had won the lottery, perhaps he would have gone back to school and become a teacher. If he had known he had so little time left on earth, perhaps he would have pursued his dream. But because my dad had very little money, and because he thought he had lots of time, he waited.

But as I grew up and became an adult, those lottery tickets my dad bought no longer spoke to me about his sadness but about his hope. After all, I'd bought lottery tickets myself hoping to get rich quick. I'd bought tickets not in a moment of desperation when I was at the end of my rope but on a lark, in a moment of wishful thinking. *Maybe I'll get lucky. Maybe I'll never have to work again.* That's what I was thinking. We all have our scratched-out lottery tickets, dreams we would be embarrassed to share with even those closest to us. So many of us are waiting for good fortune to rain down upon us. We are waiting for love, waiting for that big break, waiting for the life we want to finally begin.

Looking back at my father's death from the distance of time, I realized my dad may have had unfulfilled ambitions in work, but he was daring and courageous in love. He married the woman of his dreams, he raised four terrific children, he was a passionate and devoted family man, a loyal friend to so many. He was a leader in his synagogue community. Perhaps he wouldn't have given so much at home if he had pursued his ambitions at work.

Life involves compromise. And now I could see that my dad *did* stop waiting. He chose family over work. It was a choice he made every day. I knew it wasn't an easy one. He was willing to do unfulfilling work because that very work allowed him to live a fulfilling life at home with his wife and kids. He worked so he could put four kids through private school. He sacrificed so his children might one day be able to pursue their dreams. My dad's decision wasn't a shame or a sad waste or a loss but a choice, a really beautiful, loving choice that too many parents *don't* make.

My father was tragically cheated out of precious years he thought he still had plenty of. "Man plans and God laughs" is a bitter Yiddish proverb I was taught to say when life suddenly goes horribly wrong. We think we have control when we have no control. We make our hopeful plans oblivious to the fate that's awaiting us. And God laughs at our blindness, at our futile plans. *Poor fools.*

My father had so many plans, so many hopes for the future. He wasn't done. He was planning to change careers. Planning to move to Israel one day with my mom, the woman of his dreams. He was planning to dance at his children's weddings. Planning to bounce his grandchildren on his knee.

I had plans too. Was God laughing at me? As my rabbi friend told me with such brutal honesty over a cup of coffee, I had once been a rising star. I'd had dreams of helping people and teaching people. I'd had dreams of raising a big family with lots of kids. I had planned for my daughter to be strong and healthy. I had been blindsided. I didn't see it coming. I was a wife, a mom, a rabbi, a writer. Rob and I were deeply in love, with two beautiful children, a home, and a horrible dog. All we needed was a white picket fence. Noa was a healthy baby. Her labor took an hour. She had ten fingers and ten toes. I didn't see this coming.

Noa had plans. Like a healthy child, she imagined the future as a wide-open expanse that stretched on into eternity. I couldn't bear to think about Noa's future. It was a fog, a question mark, a mystery. Would she be with me next year? In five years? In ten?

Man plans and God laughs.

Life is exhilarating, breathtaking, and beautiful. And life is unfair and cruel, and I'd officiated over enough funerals to understand that the most important question we must ask is not what a person did for a living but what he or she did for a life. Did he have a kind heart? Did she form bonds of love? Did he live a life of meaning? Did she find joy?

My father taught me we can love and rejoice and sing even when the circumstances of our lives are less than ideal.

And one night in the middle of my waiting-room days, my father's voice called out to me from the past with a request.

I Want You to Shine

twelve

Let your face shine like the brightness
of the heavens.
The Talmud Brachot 17a

IT WAS a cold and rainy night in February and I was having trouble sleeping. The months had passed in a blur; 2002 became 2003. Noa had just turned seven. Another poignant bittersweet party was behind us. Her blond curls were a shade darker now. And though she was definitely falling down less often, she still had a long road before her. When she did fall, she lacked the proper protective reflexes. She wouldn't put out her hands to break a fall. Twice that month she fell flat on her face and both times her eyeglasses cut into her temple. Both times she needed stitches. Reactions that came as reflexes to others came to Noa through sweat and toil.

I wanted to protect her. I wanted to be her shadow, to walk before her and break every fall. I wanted to wipe out that death cloud that was hanging over our heads.

I didn't know how I would be able to wait six more years to find out whether Noa had a fatal disease or not. Time stopped.

I wished my dad could sense my helplessness. I wished he could tell me what to do. But my dad was helpless in the face of a young mugger with a gun in his hand.

I lay in bed tossing and turning. My mind racing, I decided to give up on trying to sleep. I quietly slipped out of bed and began rummaging through the old cigar box where I keep my mementos. I found a cassette tape of my dad singing to me. He made it for me when I was twelve and he was teaching me for my Bat Mitzvah. I took my cassette player off the top shelf of my closet, put in new AA batteries, and carefully loaded the tape. It was 2:00 a.m., Rob and the kids were fast asleep. I lay back on my living room couch with the cassette player on my chest and I hit play.

My dad was talking to me and teaching me how to pray. He had the loveliest, most passionate voice. I could hear his smile. I knew the sound of my dad's smile.

In the background on the tape I could hear the rhythms of my childhood home. The sound of the kitchen door swinging open. My mom was cooking dinner. My brother David's voice hadn't fully changed yet. Now I heard the phone ring; my mom was chatting happily with a friend. I could hear myself, at twelve years of age, butting in and out of different conversations.

No one on the tape could see what was coming. We were all so casual and careless. In three years my father would be murdered and we had no idea what was waiting for us. In movies there's always a sound track to warn you.

I wanted to shout into the tape recorder, "Watch out, Dad!" I wanted to tell my parents to go ahead and take that trip they'd been talking about for so long. I wanted to say to him, "Dad, if you have a dream, if you really want to do something, do it now. You've got so little time left." I wanted to tell my twelve-year-old self to treasure these sweet days with him.

At the end of the tape my dad said to me,

"Nomi, I want you to shine."

As I was lying there on the couch clutching my tape recorder I wanted to cry back, *Dad, I'm trying to shine, but I'm frightened and tired and I wish you could tell me what to do.*

No, my father would not save me. He could not save me. But his last words to me became a mantra that sustained me through my wait: *I want you to shine.* How could I learn to shine when I was living beneath a cloud of worry and uncertainty? How could I learn to embrace the imperfect present and find blessings right where I was?

I would have to learn how to see the light in the darkness. I would have to open the windows and let in the light. I would have to uncover the light flickering deep inside me. I would have to find the fuel that would cause that light to grow brighter.

The next morning Noa popped out of bed to greet me. She found me asleep on the sofa with the tape recorder in my arms. It was 6:30 a.m. and Noa jumped on me with her fairy wings. She was like Tinkerbell, all aglow. Shining came as a reflex to Noa. I would have to learn to shine through sweat and toil.

Yes, I would have to learn to shine even as I struggled to see.

thirteen

*If there's a bitterness in the heart, sugar in the mouth
won't make life sweeter.*

YIDDISH PROVERB

O NE DAY early in May, I had an hour to kill between dropping
off Adi at a gym class and picking up Noa from a playdate, and
I slipped into a small clothing boutique. I hadn't bought any clothes
for myself in quite some time. The owner of the boutique was very
helpful and kept following me around the store. For some reason,
she thought my name was Mara. She kept saying, "Mara, do you like
these jeans? Mara, can I get you another size?" When I was done
shopping I met her at the register. She asked, "How would you like
to pay for this, Mara?" I finally said to her, "Actually my name isn't
Mara, it's Naomi." She said, "I'm so sorry. I was sure your name was
Mara." I responded, "Well, actually, Mara is a part of my name, it's
the flip side of my name."

I went on to tell her about a great woman named Naomi who is
found in the Bible in the Book of Ruth. Naomi loses her husband and
her two sons and she comes back to the Land of Israel a widow, bereft
of all she once loved. The townswomen come out to greet her upon

her return, "Naomi!" The name Naomi means "sweet one." But Naomi turns to the women and says to them, "Don't call me Naomi anymore, call me Mara, 'bitter one,' because the Lord has struck out against me."

I looked at the saleswoman and explained, "So you see, you weren't so far off in calling me Mara. Mara is part of my name. It's the underside of my name." She said, "Whoa, I've got goose bumps. That's just way too freaky. I have to go sit down. That was way too heavy for me."

As I spoke those words to the saleswoman, I started to get goose bumps too. Was I turning into Mara? Could the saleswoman see the Mara in me? Could she see how bitter I had become?

The very next morning I woke up with a start to the sound of Sophie howling at a squirrel. It was 5:00 a.m., still dark outside. I walked over to my bookshelves and was immediately drawn to a biblical commentary by Rabbi Gedalyahu Schorr called *Gedalyahu's Light*. I sat down at the breakfast table, cracked open the Hebrew volume, and a mystical teaching jumped off the page whispering words of comfort.

Bad things happen to us, disappointments, hurts, and they leave their imprint on our souls. Sometimes, that imprint, that scar from our hurts, stunts our growth and prevents us from moving forward. Someone betrayed us so we have trouble trusting. Someone we loved died so we have trouble believing. Someone was cruel to us so we have trouble loving.

The mystical teaching said: Just as the hurts from our past leave an imprint on our souls, all the joys from our future leave an imprint on our souls too. The commentary said with perfect confidence that there is an imprint on our souls already from all the abundant good that is coming our way.

53

Was the imprint of future blessings already sealed on my soul?

In the realm of the spirit, past and future converge, time collapses, tomorrow's successes and celebrations have already left their mark on our souls. When all we can see are our past scars, we walk around in the present feeling hesitant, frightened, damaged, and deficient. But if we could only see the healing blessings of our future. If we could only sense all the good that awaits us, we might be more willing to take risks. We might be more open to exploring new opportunities. We might have more faith and confidence. We might have more hope.

Perhaps this mystical teaching explained how it's possible to meet a complete stranger and feel that you've known that person all your life. Maybe your souls were already connected. This teaching helped to explain why you can enter a totally new life path that doesn't feel new at all. Instead, it feels like coming home.

Could such a thing be possible? Maybe God wasn't laughing at us poor fools and our futile plans. Maybe God was trying to show us the good that was coming. Could the joys, the successes, the celebrations of the future already be inside us as we are waiting for them to unfold?

I suddenly understood that when Naomi called herself Mara, all she could see was her loss. But what she couldn't see is what every reader can see: how she becomes Naomi again, how her daughter-in-law Ruth has a child, and how that child has a child who was the father of David, King of Israel.

Yes, perhaps there were blessings coming my way; they were mine, they belonged to me. They were already wrapped up inside me. I would need to learn how to look for them, how to eagerly anticipate them, how to welcome them like gifts from above.

Perhaps blessings were coming Noa's way. Instead of worrying about a disease that was already wrapped up inside her, I could start noticing the strength that was already wrapped up inside her. Perhaps instead of preparing for the worst, I could begin anticipating the best. Yes, I convinced myself, I would live to see her blossom and grow.

I too would live to call myself Naomi again, sweet one.

That was my hope. It was my prayer, but I was having quite a bit of trouble praying.

No, I hadn't exactly stopped praying my traditional daily prayers. But I was having trouble figuring out Who I was praying to and what I was praying for.

As my prayer life was in a state of turmoil, Rob, who had always been a skeptical Jew, began making all sorts of bargains with God. I'd watch him in synagogue. It calmed me to sit beside him deep in thought. "Tell me about the rabbits, George," I'd ask him at night. I wanted to know what he believed, what he was saying to God. Rob told me, "It can't hurt to pray. I kind of put it in the same category of blowing out candles on a birthday cake. If there's anybody out there besides fate and nature, then this is what I want: LET NOA BE HEALTHY." He said he was praying to "Just In Case"—that was the name of his God. Prayer was focusing his resolve, steeling his nerves, calming him. Rob doubted Someone Up There was listening or answering. He said, "But I don't want to tempt fate. I don't pray like a believer prays, I pray like somebody who's covering his bets." He told me he believed there was a power to prayer, but he wasn't sure the Power was on the other end of the line.

Was God listening? What was the point of praying if prayer was just a monologue? I wanted to feel God. I wanted to know I wasn't alone. I couldn't pray to Just In Case, I needed to find a new name for God.

To add to the irony, at that exact time I was finishing up a book of prayers called *Talking to God*.

Yes, there were times when God's presence seemed as near to me as my own breath. And there were other times when God's very existence seemed like a mere concept—lifeless and uncertain.

I wanted desperately to talk to God from the depths of my heart, but I was paralyzed, like when you try to scream in your sleep but no sound comes out. There I was, a rabbi who had just written a book of prayers, but my spiritual life was in a state of utter turmoil. One night I confessed my crisis of faith to a colleague of mine. "At least God has a good sense of humor," he said.

Questions and answers would run through my mind: Should I ask God to make this all go away? Well, that's not very realistic, is it? Should I be angry with God? God didn't do this to Noa, nature did. Should I be grateful that Noa's condition isn't any worse? Definitely. But I still wished things were better.

The truth is, I longed to talk to God, but I was too angry to begin a conversation.

Noa and God were the best of friends, always chatting and whispering secrets.

fourteen

An angry man is not fit to pray.
YIDDISH PROVERB

ONE MORNING in early September, Noa woke up with a terrible bout of ataxia—an inability to keep her balance. If you saw her when she was having one of these attacks, she looked like someone severely drunk. Once an elderly woman stopped me on the street and told me Noa looked like a drunken sailor. It was true. Noa did wobble around like that. I would watch her teetering about with an angelic smile on her face and those fairy wings and my heart would ache. There were days when she couldn't sit upright in a chair, she'd just fall over. She couldn't walk without hitting a wall or falling down. The ataxia was always worse in the morning hours.

That morning I had to hold her up so that she could eat her breakfast without falling over. I couldn't imagine sending her to school in that condition. She wouldn't have been able to sit in her seat. So I said to her, "Honey, I don't think you should go to school today." She wouldn't hear of it. It was the second week of second grade. Noa wanted to go so badly. She said, "If I pray for a while I'll be okay."

57

She picked herself up, held on to the wall, made her way to her room, stood before the mirror, and started singing her morning prayers in Hebrew. She sang with great joy and purity. I was watching from a distance, not wanting to disturb her or make her feel self-conscious. A serenity started to flow through her body. I could see it. Her mood changed, her posture changed, her expression changed. When she was done singing, she walked straight up to me with strength and steadiness and said, "I'm ready for school now." And she was.

Prayer could do that for her.

My prayers were hollow. I'd utter the words knowing they were lies: "You lift up the fallen, heal the sick, free the captives, revive the dead."

Noa and I were on such different trajectories. She was all light. I was still Mara trying to figure out how to soften my heart.

fifteen

And I will remove the heart of stone from you,
and I will give you a heart of flesh.
EZEKIEL 36:26

EVERY NIGHT Rob and I went through the same bedtime ritual with Noa. I'd crawl into bed with her first and sing a James Taylor lullaby. He had written the song for his daughter Sarah Maria; I changed the name for my daughter Noa Rakia. Noa means "something in motion." Rakia means "heaven." Then Rob would join us in bed and sing the cowboy song "Red River Valley" to Noa and then Noa would sing the traditional Jewish bedtime prayer called the Shema, "Listen Israel, the Lord our God, the Lord is One."

One night I climbed into bed with Noa and sang my song, "Well, the moon is in the ocean and the stars are in the sky, but all that I can see are my sweet Rakia's eyes . . ." Thinking of the moon in the ocean calmed me. I imagined a full moon reflected on the face of the sea by night. There was magic to it. The heavens were smiling on the earth. All would be well. When I was done singing, Noa called out to Rob to tell him it was his turn and he hopped on the bed and sang, "Come and sit by my side if you love me, do not hasten to bid me adieu, just remember the Red River Valley and the cowboy who loves you so true." At some point during his singing, Sophie jumped on Noa's bed too and began burrowing under the covers. And as the three of us prayed the Shema together lying on Noa's bed in the dark with Sophie squirming away between us, my heart started to soften. For an instant I could see what a blessed life I had.

When the heart is closed, nothing can get in.

The Shema we had just prayed told us to "Love the Lord your God with all your heart, with all your soul, with all your might." And then it said, "Place the words I command you today on your heart." A Hasidic master, Rabbi Levi Yitzhak of Berditchev, once asked, "Why are we commanded to put the words *on* our hearts? Shouldn't we put them *in* our hearts?" His answer: Sometimes the heart is closed and it can't take the words in. Our job is to simply put the words on our hearts.

When the heart is ready, it will open and the words will seep in like water on parched land.

Yes, I understood this intellectually, but I wondered, when would my heart be ready to receive the words of hope that were sitting on it?

Luminous Days

s i x t e e n

If things are not as you wish, wish them as they are.
YIDDISH PROVERB

I WAS driving a rental car trying to find my way to a rehabilitation center. That October, Rob and I had planned to take Adi and Noa to visit my mom, but my mom fell and developed a terrible wound that just wouldn't heal. First she was in the hospital and then she was transferred to a rehabilitation unit for a month. She'd been stuck in bed and unable to stand or walk or to go outside all that time. I had flown to Boston alone to be with her.

It was a beautiful October day, but I was feeling blue for my mom. As I was sitting there with her in the rehab she fell asleep, so I quietly tiptoed out and drove to a pond nearby called Jamaica Pond. I hadn't been back east in October in a really long time. And the leaves! I'd forgotten what fall was like. The leaves were on fire with colors and I started walking around this pond surrounded by the leaves and the trees and the water.

Suddenly I stopped and picked up a single leaf, a bright red leaf. Then I walked a little more and I picked up a stick and I remembered what it was like when Adi was little and he would pick up a stick and that stick could be anything—it could be a gun, a conductor's baton, or a fishing rod. I was walking and waving my stick that could be anything and holding my leaf and then I picked up another leaf that was bright yellow. I was so moved by how beautiful it was, so sunny and bright.

Sometimes you're in such a powerful zone of presence and connectedness that you become a magnet. People started to come up to me, strangers. A Latino man saw me and he looked at me and said, "Here, you'll like this one." And he handed me a bright orange leaf. Kids started following me and collecting leaves and giving me leaves.

I kept walking with these beautiful leaves in my hand. And I had an epiphany, one of those flashes that are so rare in life. I flashed to my own Bat Mitzvah. I started to remember when I was twelve how my father taught me the Haftorah, how to chant a reading from the Prophets, and he taught me how to pray and lead a prayer service. And I remembered how he fought so hard to force my synagogue to allow a girl to lead the prayer service. Of course, they fought back. They didn't want to let a girl lead even one prayer. They had all sorts of excuses, but he was more determined and he was more unrelenting and they gave in. My Bat Mitzvah was the first time in my synagogue that they ever let a girl lead a single prayer in Hebrew.

And at my Bat Mitzvah my mom cooked the entire festive meal for our whole community. She cooked everything. All the food for hundreds of people. All the chicken, all the casseroles, all the cakes. The food was stored all across Brooklyn. All of her friends had the food for my Bat Mitzvah stored in their refrigerators and in their freezers. Everywhere around town there was Naomi's Bat Mitzvah food. And instead of flowers for my Bat Mitzvah, for centerpieces she and all her friends collected fall leaves. Bright, beautiful fall leaves for every table.

At that age I was embarrassed. All the other kids in my grade had Bar or Bat Mitzvahs that were big affairs, fancy parties in fancy halls with bands and caterers and waiters all dressed in black and white. And my Bat Mitzvah was this homespun thing and my mom's friends all waited the tables in their dresses and their pearls. Just then as I was feeling particularly ashamed, the richest kid in our class, his name was Scott Zipes and he lived on Shore Road right by the water, he came up to me and said, "Gosh, Naomi, I've never seen such well-dressed help at any Bar Mitzvah I've ever been to."

This was my epiphany as I was standing at the pond surrounded by leaves and strangers and the stick that could be anything: I suddenly realized just how beautiful my Bat Mitzvah was. A prayer service led by a father who had taught his daughter well how to pray and how to fight against prejudice and injustice. A Shabbat dinner cooked with love, served by friends, with tables adorned and illuminated with the bounty of the fall leaves in bright reds and oranges and yellows.

I took all the leaves I gathered that day at the pond and I took the stick that could be anything and I taped all the leaves together in a bundle around it until it became a beautiful bouquet. Then I put the bouquet in an empty wine bottle and brought it to my mom's room in the rehab.

And there we ate a homespun Shabbat dinner together in her room. Our makeshift table was on fire with the beauty of a fall day and the gratitude of a mother and a daughter for all the blessings of today.

When I got home from Boston, I could see something was beginning to shift inside me. Yes, Noa was still struggling. Yes, it was all so unfair. Yes, there was that question mark hanging over our heads. But I was beginning to see the blessings of the moment. I wasn't thinking "If only"—everything would be perfect *if only* we could be certain Noa was healthy. Once when I was a child whining to my mother about the unfairness of some situation, she taught me this Yiddish proverb: "If my grandmother had whiskers she'd be my grandfather." And just to raise my spirits she taught me the racier version too: "If my grandmother had testicles she'd be my grandfather." The lesson was simple: You can't live your life wishing things were different than they are.

The truth is, things were ambiguous and scary and they were also wonderful.

Rob was cooking a sumptuous dinner and sipping a glass of red wine. Adi was tackling Noa and tickling her. She was giggling and screaming. I jumped on Adi and started tickling him. Rob jumped on me. Of course, Sophie burrowed in somewhere. For a moment, the bitter taste left my tongue. The sound of my kids' laughter was sweet manna from heaven.

Later that night as I stood at the sink washing the dishes, words my father had once taught me seeped into my heart.

When I was preparing for my Bat Mitzvah, my father taught me to chant a section from the second Book of Kings. It's a story about a poor widow who comes crying to a prophet named Elisha who is a miracle worker. The widow tells Elisha her sad story: Her husband is dead and she owes money to a sadistic collector who wants to take her two boys away and keep them as his slaves if she doesn't pay up. Elisha's not worried. He says, "What do you have at home?" She says, "Nothing . . . except for a small bottle of oil." He tells her to go borrow all sorts of pots and pans from her neighbors. She does. When she comes back to Elisha he says, "Now start pouring that oil." Sure enough, the oil in her one little bottle keeps flowing. It fills up every pot and pan, every bucket and barrel she can find. She comes back to Elisha and he says, "Now go sell your oil. You and your boys will have enough to live on for the rest of your days."

I didn't really understand this story when I was a kid, and I certainly didn't understand it when I was an adult feeling angry and empty. I thought it was just a legend about a miracle worker. But now, standing at the sink, I could see that the Prophet Elisha, who lived two thousand years ago, was talking to me, he was talking to all the people who couldn't see what treasures they had. He was telling me I had more blessings, more potential, more strength than I thought. And all of that abundance wasn't waiting for me in some far-off land or some distant time. The treasures were already here with me, in side me, all around me. How could I learn to uncover them and rejoice in them?

For too long I'd spent my time fearing the worst. Even thinking about my own Bat Mitzvah filled me with heartache because I so wanted Noa to have a Bat Mitzvah, I so wanted to teach her the way my father had taught me. But I was told I had to wait until Noa was thirteen to find out if she was going to degenerate or not.

I wanted to stop worrying and brooding and feeling helpless and cursed. What did I have at home? So much to be grateful for. A husband who was my soul mate, two incredible, amazing children, an adorable dog who was always destroying things, a roof over our heads, food in our kitchen, clothing in our closets.

What did I have? My mother, my sister, my brothers, my in-laws. I had true friends who were always there to listen, to help, to lift me up when I was down. I had rabbi friends whom I could lean on for wisdom and support. I had wonderful neighbors, the Lipkis family, and the Wilands, who had become dear friends, with a little girl named Winona who had become Noa's best friend. I loved watching these two blond beauties giggle and run around the backyard and make a mess of my kitchen.

"What do you have at home?" I whispered to myself as I crawled into bed beside Rob, who was already fast asleep. The words felt good in my heart.

The next morning I went to Starbucks to study Torah with my friend Toba, also a rabbi. We had recently become Chevrutah partners, study buddies. A Chevrutah is someone you study religious texts with on a regular basis. If you're lucky, your Chevrutah can occupy a sacred role in your life. It's someone who leads you deeper into thought, someone who questions your assumptions. When two people fit together well, they can raise each other up to spiritual heights that neither one of them could have reached alone. A good Chevrutah is hard to find. There has to be just the right kind of chemistry. And when you get a Chevrutah that works, it's such a gift.

Friday mornings with Toba at 7:30 a.m. at Starbucks anchored my week. I eagerly looked forward to every one of our sessions. With Toba I'd leave my day "job" behind (the worried mother in the waiting room) and enter the world of the Torah. That day we came upon a verse in the Bible I had never thought about in quite that way before.

seventeen

Eating nothing but dumplings is also boring.
YIDDISH PROVERB

TOBA AND I sat down at our usual table at Starbucks by the window. A Ray Charles song was playing, "Unchain My Heart." People kept eavesdropping on us, trying to figure out what language we were speaking as we read aloud in Hebrew. We were discussing the miracle of manna. The Bible describes manna as a substance that fell down like dew when the Children of Israel were wandering in the desert. Manna was nourishment from God in the barren wilderness.

Suddenly we came upon a verse in Deuteronomy that described manna in a new way. Moses tells the people, "God sent you manna in order to test you."

I'd never thought about manna as a test. I'd always thought about it as a divine gift.

Immediately I understood what the test was.

On Day 1 manna looks like a real miracle. On Day 2 manna still seems quite miraculous. On Day 30 manna is getting seriously boring. By Day 60 manna seems like some sort of punishment.

The manna test was the test of normal. Every miracle, if you're blessed and lucky enough so that it lasts in your life and you get to keep it, becomes normal. And then it doesn't seem like such a miracle.

I turned to Toba and said, "I have so much manna in my life, why isn't it filling me up?"

Toba kept telling me how lucky I was, how blessed I was, how blessed Noa was. She reminded me how happy Noa was, how beautiful she was, how good she was, how wise. I tried my best to take this all in, though the Ray Charles song perfectly fit my mood, "Unchain My Heart." My heart was still feeling locked up.

One of my favorite blessings in all of the rabbinic writings is, "May you see your world in your lifetime." I think it means, may you experience the bliss of the World to Come in this world.

In *Paths of Peace* I read a powerful explanation of this blessing that said if you can't experience your World to Come in this life, then when you get to the next world you won't be able to experience it there either. A person who is bored and blind and frustrated in this world will be fated to become a bench in the Garden of Eden. Everyone else will be enjoying the magnificent garden and you'll be the bench they sit on when they need to rest.

I didn't want to be a bench. And yet I felt like I had become a bench, sitting around all day in waiting rooms praying that this doctor or that therapist would miraculously "fix" Noa.

I read further and came upon another insight about seeing your world in your lifetime. When a revered Hasidic rabbi was on his deathbed, he began to weep. His disciples surrounded him, "Rabbi, what's the matter?" He said, "I just had the most beautiful insight. I saw my whole life pass before me. The days I thought were luminous were actually quite ordinary. And the days I thought were ordinary were actually the most luminous of all."

Was that possible? Could these days in the waiting rooms be the most luminous days of all? What was I missing? Why couldn't I see any light except for those industrial fluorescent tubes shining down on me and making my skin look green?

eighteen

It is not good to be alone, even in Paradise.
YIDDISH PROVERB

Now it was a Friday afternoon and I was sitting with Noa in the waiting room before her physical therapy session. Noa and a few other kids were playing at the plastic Fisher-Price table that stood in the center of the room. I was listening to one of the moms telling us that she had taken legal action against the LA school district and won! We were all so happy for her. Her success gave us all hope that one day we might win our battles against the district as well.

Could it be that the waiting rooms were luminous places? There were kids with cancer, kids with cerebral palsy, kids with autism, kids with amputated limbs, kids who had been born prematurely. And they were all so beautiful. In their daily lives these kids stood out, they had developmental delays, they were teased, they were picked last for every team at PE, some awful teacher was always burying them in the back row of every school performance. But in the waiting rooms no child stood out, no one was special. Everyone special was normal.

And the parents, we didn't have to fend off pity in the waiting rooms. We didn't have to pretend all was fine in the waiting rooms. We could share dark humor. We could share wisdom learned by experience. We could ask questions we would never dare ask anyone else. We could warn newcomers to avoid a certain doctor who was cold or cruel. And we could comfort one another.

There were twin boys, about eighteen months old, who graced the waiting room with their mother every single week. One had blond hair and one had brown hair. This mom had her hands full. Two boys with cerebral palsy who both had significant disabilities. And yet she was always so patient, so loving, so positive, and so calm. The twins shared an incredible bond, but the one with brown hair was stronger than the one with blond hair.

One night the weaker twin died in his crib. And now this grieving mother appeared with her only son. The waiting room became a place of tears, of comfort and support. The boy who lived seemed lost without his brother, uncomfortable to have to brave this world solo.

No one wants to brave this world solo. That's why the waiting room was such a luminous place.

We had each other.

And then there was Evalina.

nineteen

There is hope for your future, says the Lord.
JEREMIAH 31:16

EVALINA RICCI. Her name sounded like a fine wine. She had long red hair and a smile that made everyone in the waiting room smile. Evalina was Noa's physical therapist. She'd peek into the waiting room, call out to Noa, and Noa would come running to her. Evalina worked Noa hard. She worked her and worked her some more and she had that rare way of making the most grueling exercise seem like the most exciting adventure. The very first day she assessed Noa, she looked me in the eye and said, "This girl is tough."

The therapists at this clinic were overworked and underpaid and they looked it. It's not easy to work with children who have disabilities all day. You have to deal with so many temper tantrums and tears and screams and snotty noses. But Evalina was all smiles always. She had a natural instinct for turning work into play, a struggle into a game. With her there was a jungle to enter, a river to cross, Beanie Babies instead of balls. She saw the best in every child and got the best out of every child.

What was it about Evalina that filled her with so much light? She had every reason to be frustrated and burned out. What she saw every day was so unfair. Innocent kids with so many struggles. Innocent kids who were missing limbs, kids who were deformed, kids who couldn't speak, kids who were paralyzed. How could she be so upbeat all the time?

What was in the water she was drinking and how could I get some? Evalina got married and then got pregnant and she continued to work with Noa and had the same contagious energy even when her belly was as big as the therapy ball she was balancing Noa on.

When I watched Noa struggling to keep up with other kids, when my heart would break for her, I'd repeat Evalina's assessment: "This girl is tough."

Evalina saw hope. She saw the positive even in the negative. She saw strength when others saw weakness. I wanted to learn to see hope. And that's when my friend Ari called.

twenty

*If you can't endure the bad, you won't live
to see the good.*
YIDDISH PROVERB

I WAS sitting in the window seat on a plane to Philadelphia. I could
see the reflection of my face in the glass. It was November 2003.
"The years haven't been too cruel to me," I thought. I wondered if
Ari would agree. I worried about how Ari would look. He'd been
through so much that year.

I'd known Ari since we were both teenagers playing guitar in
summer camp, and strangely enough, we both grew up to become
rabbis. Several months earlier Ari had phoned me to tell me he had
been diagnosed with a rare blood disease. He had gone for a simple
physical to renew his driver's license and his doctor discovered an
abnormality in his blood proteins. Soon he flew to Boston and went
through high-dose chemotherapy followed by a stem-cell transplant.
Ari told me they call the day of your stem-cell transplant your birthday. It's the day when new life begins. Ari phoned me excitedly about
a month after the procedure. He said, "Nomi, it *is* like being reborn,
the hair on my face is coming in not all scratchy like a man's but like
peach fuzz, the way it did when I was a Bar Mitzvah boy." And then

came the wait to see whether his protein levels had returned to normal. They were normal. And then came the continuing wait, the hope that the disorder would remain in long-term remission.

And now I was heading back east to spend the Sabbath with Ari and his family. Ari met me at the airport; we hugged and drove to his home. I was relieved to see him looking just as I had remembered him. It was wonderful to see him healthy, surrounded by his wife and his kids. He was training to run a marathon. We ate festive Sabbath meals, sang old songs we used to sing as children; we shared memories and laughed until we cried late into the night.

On Saturday night I stopped laughing and I asked Ari, "Tell me, what have you learned from your illness?" Ari smiled and changed the subject.

The next morning when I awoke there was a letter on my bed. Ari had stayed up most of the night writing to me:

A simple question, which demands a well-thought-out answer. Learning is never simple or direct. It could take years to discover what we have learned. Perhaps I have yet to discover the true meaning of the question. And so, this is only the start of a very long answer. Maybe you will ask the same question of me every year. I'll fly to Boston and the doctors will ask their questions, and you my friend will ask your question. And their questions will always be the same: "How do you feel?" "Have there been any significant changes since we last examined you?" And your question will always be the same: "What did you learn from your illness?"

Ari wrote to me about the hour just before dusk, about the stars and the moon and the sunrise. He wrote about the incredible display of fall colors and the clear ice that envelops the thin branches of the trees on a frost-filled morning. He called death "the pursuer, whose dark breath I felt running down my neck." He spoke about his wife's soft skin, the depth in her eyes, and his favorite sound in the world— the sound of his kids' voices. He talked about finding God in moments of quiet. He said he learned how unbelievable the human body is; he was awed by its capacity to cure itself. He said a great lesson he learned from illness was to take care of himself. He was learning to be kind to himself, learning not to judge himself, learning to make time to rest, learning to make time for having fun, learning to make time for doing the things he loved. He ended his letter saying, "My biggest lesson is patience. It's the most important thing in the world. And we're so impatient."

I once read a quote from Václav Havel, who said in a speech to the U.S. Congress: "A person who cannot move and lead a somewhat normal life because he is pinned under a boulder has more time to think about his hopes than someone who is not trapped that way."

On my flight back home I reread Ari's letter. I told myself there is a period in every person's life when one must travel through the desert. Yes, it would be nice to get to the Promised Land already, but the only way to get there is through that vast desert that seems to stretch on as far as your eyes can see. The Children of Israel spent forty years wandering in the desert. But it was in the desert that they found their strength and their faith. It was there in the middle of the vast wilderness where they received God's word that would nourish and sustain them. Yes, they were parched and they endured blistering heat, but they found grace in the wilderness.

As I was waiting for my daughter to get stronger, waiting for life to begin, I had imagined I was stuck in Bo's whale. But now I was starting to see . . . maybe I hadn't been stuck at all. Perhaps I'd been slowly traveling through a wilderness. And though the landscape looked the same each day, I had certainly been moving forward. I was not always able to see my progress, but I had already traveled a long distance from my place of blindness and entrapment.

I love the hopeful words of the Prophet Jeremiah, who said, "The people who survived the sword found grace in the wilderness." It was possible to find grace in the wilderness. During those uncertain days, I would sing that verse to myself and try to believe.

Ari taught me I must be patient with myself as I journeyed.

Luminous days. Was I beginning to experience them?

I couldn't write or work or pray. But I could mommy. Was my spiritual and professional paralysis helping me to be a better mother to my children? I had nothing pulling me away from them. No outside concerns or commitments. My sense of time was beginning to shift. I was no longer watching the clock or rushing them because of some schedule I needed to keep. I even stopped carrying a calendar. I turned down requests for teaching and lecturing, I stopped attending seminars and meetings. I was officially out of the loop. To my colleagues I was one of those promising rabbis who gave it all up to be a mom. But was something sacred unfolding inside me?

I was feeling compassion for people I had once judged. I was learning to be more patient with myself and less frustrated. Was I stronger than I had imagined? I was learning that Noa was tough and resilient and blessed in ways I was just beginning to understand. I was learning to rethink my priorities and ambitions. I was learning that I was not alone, that I could lean on others for help and that I could help others even when I felt weak and lost and confused myself. I was learning about love, about true friends, and about hope and endurance. I was learning to see blessings where I once saw curses. I was beginning to understand that the wait doesn't ever really end— the closer you get to the Promised Land, the farther away it seems. Just when you think you've finally "gotten there," you realize how much more journeying there is to do.

When I got home from the airport there was a denial letter from our insurance company waiting for me on the dining room table. They were officially cutting off Noa's coverage for her physical and occupational therapies. I was fuming and pacing. This was not the first battle I'd had to wage to get Noa the treatments she so desperately needed. Every few months I fought a new battle with the school district or California Children's Services or the regional center or the insurance company. Every provider argued that some other organization should be funding Noa's therapies and services. Our health insurer sent us to the school district, the school district sent us to California Children's Services, CCS sent us to the regional center, the regional center sent us back to our health insurer. Each one of these battles required a whole new barrage of letters for us to write, and letters of support from Noa's various doctors, and a whole new battery of tests and assessments for Noa to go through. And then there were the countless phone calls, the eternal maze of automated operators and waiting on hold.

So much for all those lessons I thought I had learned. Yes, Ari had taught me to see that I wasn't trapped in Bo's whale, but it didn't take much to set me back. That denial letter sent me on a tailspin. I felt like I was drowning all over again. I couldn't see my way out of the waves that kept tossing me from here to there. Then I remembered that Ari had told me the biggest lesson was patience. With patience could I find a way to pull myself out of the water again?

twenty-one

You can't control the wind,
but you can adjust your sails.

YIDDISH PROVERB

I'D HAD such an incredible weekend with Ari and now I was spending hours on the phone trying to fight the denial letter from our insurance company. I was pacing back and forth in our hallway. The customer service agent repeated the company's position: They didn't think Noa needed any more physical therapy. I was pleading. I asked to speak to a supervisor. I was left on hold again for more than half an hour, but I didn't dare hang up. It had taken me so long to get this far. I had memorized the loop of Muzak songs they play you when you're on hold. Right then I was suffering through a really lame version of "Let It Be" on the saxophone. I knew when that maddening recording was going to come on and trick you into thinking you'd finally gotten a live person.

How long can you wait on hold? I thought to myself. I wanted to write. I wanted to study. I wanted to teach, work, help people. I wanted to have a baby. We always thought we'd have four kids. But Noa's doctors discouraged us from having more kids right away. It was selfish to want to bring another child into the world who might have a fatal disease. WAIT.

My life will begin when . . . That's what I told myself as I was waiting on hold. *My life will begin when we hear that Noa is going to be fine. My life will begin when Noa has no more disabilities. My life will begin when Noa is done with therapies. My life will begin when we can have another baby. My life will begin when I start writing again. My life will begin when I start working again. My life will begin when . . .*

I could see the ways I'd been promising myself there was a heaven waiting for me. And just then something snapped inside my soul: *This IS my heaven.* I'd been walking around thinking, "This isn't my life, my life is coming, it's just around the bend." I started thinking of all the people I knew who were chanting the very same line.

Suddenly I could see there was a whole tribe of people just like me and we were all caught in the same lie. We were fooling ourselves into thinking our lives hadn't yet begun.

But none of us were fetuses in the womb, and we weren't ghosts either, we were people who had to learn to LIVE inside the imperfect lives we had. That didn't mean we had to stop dreaming and praying and working for things to improve. But it did mean we had to stop settling for Muzak.

Suddenly I shouted into the phone, "I don't want to live my life on hold!" And I hung up.

I still had the turntable I took with me to college and all my old records. I walked away from the phone, carefully pulled out *Let It Be*, placed the needle on the vinyl, cranked up the volume, and sang at the top my lungs.

. . . there is still a light that shines on me, shine until tomorrow, let it be.

Where Am I?

twenty - two

And the Lord God called to Adam, and said to him,
Where are you?

GENESIS 3:9

I T WAS a winter day like all others, sunny and warm in Los Ange-les. It was December 2003. I woke up, gave the kids some Honey Nut Cheerios for breakfast, and drove them both to school. I was driving back home when I heard three words. At first they approached me in a whisper; soon the voice got louder. The words echoed through me all week when I was driving carpool, when I was lying in bed at night, when I was standing in the shower. The words kept beckoning me. Those three little words took me on a ride: *Where am I?*

A voice was calling me back to myself. I'd come untethered, I'd forgotten my strengths. I'd ignored my blessings. I'd lost sight of my promise. My fear had overtaken my faith. The voice started tug-ging on my shirtsleeve, tapping me on the shoulder, pulling me by the hand. It was persistent, that voice in my head. I started answer-ing it. *I'm here. I'm a rabbi. I'm a frightened mother. I'm a child of God. I'm a wife. I'm a writer. I'm tired of waiting. I'm ready to step inside my life. I can do this. It will require boldness, abandon, tenacity.*

I understood that sooner or later we all find ourselves asking this question: Where am I? For some it's a passing blip that invades their thoughts when their defenses are down. For others it's a full-blown cry accompanied by agitation, melancholy, weariness, sleeplessness, and loneliness.

I knew there were many ways to view this period of existential questioning. A therapist might look upon it as a sign of emotional turmoil: the confusion of youth, a midlife crisis, a symptom of depression. A career counselor might view it as an expression of burnout, a need for a new job or a new career. A physician might search for signs of illness. An interior designer might say it was time for a home remodel.

But I was sure a sage would say: It's the beginning of a journey.

So where was I going?

By some strange coincidence, I was reading a book called *The Thirteen Petalled Rose* by Adin Steinsaltz at that time. The last chapter of the book is a mystical interpretation of the question "Where am I?"

How weird was that?

Rabbi Steinsaltz was talking about the relationship between heaven and earth. He said heaven mirrors earth. I tried to imagine the mirroring of a Rorschach inkblot and then I thought of Mirror Lake in Yosemite National Park. I started to picture heaven and earth as parallel dimensions. I visualized Jacob's dream of the ladder with angels ascending and angels descending. And then I remembered Noa's lullaby, "The moon is in the ocean." Yes, yes, there was the moon above, that perfect life I was yearning for, and then there was the moon below, the uncertain yet magical life I was actually living. And these two worlds were connected?

Now Rabbi Steinsaltz was saying that my question "Where am I?" also had its mirror in the world above. The first question God asked Adam in the Garden of Eden was: "Where are you?" Perhaps God didn't ask this question only one time in history to only one person. What if it was a question that was echoing through eternity? God was always asking it to every person. *Where are you? Why are you hiding? Why aren't you living up to your potential? Why can't you see how blessed you are, how loved you are?*

What if the question "Where am I?" that I'd been asking myself came from God? What if God had been calling out to me "Where are you?" and my soul had been hearing that question and asking "Where am I?" That's what Rabbi Steinsaltz was saying. Even though people often feel alone when they start asking this question, it's actually a double calling. God calling out: "Where are you?" followed by the soul's cry: "Where am I?"

Where are you?
Where am I?

So maybe God wasn't Bernard, the camp counselor who paddled away from me in the storm. Maybe God was whispering to my soul. Maybe God was as close to me as my own breath.

Every time I found myself asking "Where am I?" I tried to imagine God asking me "Where are you?" It might be easy to dismiss the question if it was coming from my own head. But what if God had been desperately trying to wake me up?

Was such a thing even possible? Could Bernard, the God who left me drowning, actually be trying to reach me?

twenty-three

I lifted up my eyes, and looked, and behold, a certain man clothed in linen.

DANIEL 10:5

I WAS walking on Venice Beach one morning passing by a homeless woman who reeked of urine and was talking to herself. I couldn't decide if she was psychotic or drunk. Then again, I'd been having some pretty strange experiences of my own lately. Was it possible that God was calling me? That God was calling everybody all the time? What did God want from me? Asking that particular question was something of a sore point for me. It called to mind a pretty unusual night. A night that taught me I wasn't exactly ready to learn what God wanted from me.

In the spring of 1990, when I first became a rabbi, it was the second night of Passover and I had just led the most elevated seder of my life. It was a community seder at my temple in Venice. I can't really put into words what happened that night. It's too hard to define. All I can say is that it was an evening full of so much joy and light. Every person there that night was part of that light. We could all feel it. When the seder was over, I walked home from the temple in such a heightened state. I could see that I had a unique gift for lifting people up, but I wasn't exactly sure where to take them. Then I lay down in bed and prayed to God for a sign. I prayed, "What do You want from me?" And I looked up—and there was a figure floating above me. Right above the whole length of me. It was shrouded in white strips of cloth. Here and there strips were fluttering in the air above me. The white strips looked like . . . toilet paper. I couldn't see the figure's face. I couldn't tell if it was a man or a woman. I was petrified. I didn't know what I had called up. Was it an angel? The soul of my father, of blessed memory? Was it the Angel of Death?

I closed my eyes to make it go away, I opened them and it was still there. I closed my eyes again and said, "Please, God, make it go away." I opened my eyes and it was still there. I closed my eyes again and this time I said, "Please, God, I'm not ready for this." I opened my eyes and it was gone. I closed my eyes again and was afraid to reopen them. And I went to sleep.

The next day I met Rob, my future husband, for a walk on the beach. He was only my boyfriend then. I was a little scared to tell him what had happened the night before. We were just dating. I didn't want him to think I was psychotic. I told him all about this "encounter" I'd had. I asked him, "What was it? Was it a dream? A nightmare? A vision? Who was it? What did it want from me?" Rob said, "Nomi, if God could come to Moses in a burning bush, who's to say that God can't come to you in a roll of Charmin?"

It's not every day that an angel comes to you in a roll of toilet paper . . . I needed time to make sense of this. And then one Friday, fourteen years after my toilet-paper vision, as I was studying at Starbucks with Toba, we came upon this story in the Talmud: Rabbi Joshua, son of Levi, has a mystical encounter with Elijah the Prophet and asks him, "When will the Messiah come?" Elijah replies, "Go and ask him yourself." "Where is he?" Joshua asks. "He sits at the entrance to the city gates," Elijah replies. "And how will I be able to recognize him?" Joshua asks. "He is sitting among the poor lepers: All of them untie their bandages all at once and then rebind them all, but the Messiah is the only leper who unties and rebinds only one sore at a time, thinking, *I must be prepared to save the world at a moment's notice.*"

That morning I told Toba the story of my angel dressed in toilet paper. And we both had the same thought: Maybe the leper in white bandages was my angel dressed in toilet paper. Maybe this is what my angel dressed in toilet paper was trying to tell me that night so many years before. I had asked God, "What do You want from me?" And God's answer to my question was: "I want you to look for the Messiah among the lepers, I want you to find salvation in the places where you normally avert your gaze."

It was Friday morning and that night Toba would be delivering a sermon to her congregation. Even though I had no pulpit and no sermon to deliver that evening, I found myself writing out this sermon to myself on a Starbucks napkin:

I do believe that's what God wants from me and from all people. And it's such a hard mission to fulfill. We all want the blessings, not the sweat and toil. We get so caught up in our own thoughts and in our own blindness, in our own troubles and in our own comforts, that we can't see how much we are needed. But perhaps working to see the Messiah among the lepers is our salvation.

In the Psalms it says, "The stone the builders discarded has become the cornerstone." Right now there may be something we are discarding that could be the very foundation of our happiness. Maybe it's not status-bearing enough, maybe it's not cool enough, maybe it doesn't pay enough. Maybe it doesn't feed our egos enough. But it may have the power to nourish and sustain our souls. The Messiah may be hiding among the lepers just waiting to be noticed.

Yes, we're sometimes lost and searching for direction, but right here, right in front of us, maybe there's an angel dressed in toilet paper who is trying to get our attention and show us the way to blessings and to clarity.

If we listen, maybe the obstacles before us will begin to melt. Maybe the path before us can become clear, and the heart of stone inside us will become a heart of flesh. Maybe that light within us will grow brighter, and will begin to shine and illuminate the places we enter. Maybe we will no longer feel cut off and separated from the world. Maybe we will begin to see unity, to see beyond our small world.

For the first time, in a very long time, we will feel alive.

An angel in toilet paper, a sermon on a napkin. A perfect fit.

I took my napkin with me and reread it as I packed my suitcase and packed the kids up for a trip to visit our friend Jack who used to live on our block.

twenty - four

What soap is to the body, laughter is to the soul.
YIDDISH PROVERB

ARE WE there yet?" Adi and Noa took turns asking us from the backseat of our rental car. As we made our way to Jack's house, the landscape around us grew lush and peaceful. A year earlier, Jack had gotten tired of waiting for his life to begin. Jack is a screenwriter who worried he was wasting years wondering how and if he'd get another movie made. After a trip to Vancouver and the Pacific Northwest, Jack impulsively sold his Santa Monica home and moved to a house by a lake in a university town near the Canadian border. Rob and I couldn't believe Jack traded his city life and volleyball at the beach for deer and bunnies hopping around his yard. We decided we needed to go visit him.

It was the weekend just after Thanksgiving when we arrived in Jack's little town, and Rob just couldn't resist making reservations at a B&B called The Beagle. I was so looking forward to getting away from home, to leaving the world of carpools and therapies and waiting rooms behind me. When we got to The Beagle, one of the owners greeted us at the door and she took us on a tour of the place. There were four beagles running around, one of them in diapers. And beagle knickknacks everywhere we turned. Beagle pillows, beagle figurines, beagle portraits. I opened the closet and there were beagle slippers on the floor for us to wear. Of course, the kids loved the place, especially those slippers.

The two things I liked most about The Beagle were an outdoor hot tub under the stars and the fact that we were the only guests.

That night we went out for pizza with Jack. He seemed reinvigorated by his move, more alive and more at peace with himself. He was working with his hands, installing floor-to-ceiling windows with a spectacular view of all that nature. Jack said he wasn't sure how this rustic thing would play out. Some nights his dog, Luna, would catch a whiff of something unknown or scary and wonder about their new venture. Jack told us he knew the feeling, but it still felt good to shake things up.

When we got back to The Beagle, we put the kids to bed and the owners came by to tell us they were going to bed as well. At around 11:00 p.m. Rob remembered the outdoor hot tub under the stars.

"Nomi, we just have to go in."

"But I don't have a swimsuit. Do you?"

"No, but who cares. There's no one here but us."

"Okay, then."

We both got into the hot tub and it was positively magical. The sky was lit up with more stars than I had ever seen in my life. We were sitting there basking in the brilliance of it all—and suddenly we heard footsteps. Three flashlight beams were moving toward us. There were three people coming at us and we were naked. What did we do? We froze, curled up in a ball, and sank down in the tub. As they got closer we saw it was a husband, a wife, and their son, who was about ten. As they approached us, they set off the motion sensor and now there were floodlights shining on us. We were all curled up in a ball and they walked right up to us with their flashlights pointing at us and we exchanged a seriously uncomfortable "Hi." They kept going, but that kid kept turning back. The father came back and forth a few more times and set off the floodlights each time he passed us. The expression on his face said, "These people are perverts." Then again, with all that walking back and forth, perhaps he was the pervert. Rob and I were laughing. I said, "Well, we'll never see them again."

The next morning, I heard a noise outside our bedroom. I listened more carefully. It was laughter. My kids were playing with the kid who saw more of us than he expected in the hot tub. A few minutes later we were all being called in for breakfast. I forgot that breakfast at a B&B is a social event. We were going to have to see those people again. I sat down at the table. The father was staring at me. Actually, he was glaring. I could feel his eyes on me. What was he thinking? I didn't look up. This went on for quite some time. He was staring at me, I was looking down picking at a blueberry muffin, then he said, "Rabbi Levy! You spoke at the Torah dedication at our temple."

Rob and I broke into a laughing jag. I was laughing so hard that tears were just rolling down my cheeks. After breakfast I went back to our room, sat in the rocking chair, and sighed the way you do after a laugh that leaves you feeling weak and emptied out. As I was rocking and sighing, I had a flash of insight: *My life might be on pause, but there is cause for laughter. Noa may or may not have a fatal disease, but right now she's flopping around happily in beagle slippers. And that's cause for celebration. Adi is busy building a Lego castle with the kid whose mind I think I warped. There might be a dark cloud hanging over our heads, but at least it's shady here. I might be a falling star, but my father told me to shine, so I want to shine brightly even as I descend.*

I wanted to get naked all over again. Not literally. I wanted to do something unexpected. I wanted to free myself from my state of paralysis. I was ready to break down the walls, escape from my land of seclusion. I would stop being Noa's taskmaster, I would stop dragging her to every possible therapy. We would play and sing and flap our fairy wings.

Soon I began thinking about a different kind of naked—the truth. A naked truth I admitted to myself about mothering Noa: I couldn't fix Noa. But I could help her. I could raise her to be strong. I could love her. I could guide her. She already knew, far better than I did, how to shine.

I suddenly understood the naked truth about my own paralysis: I was so scared of losing Noa that I couldn't see straight anymore.

I'd forgotten that I had gifts and talents to share with other people. I'd forgotten that I was a good rabbi who could teach and counsel and help people pray. I couldn't remember how to write. A mentor of mine told me to take notes on everything that had been going on with Noa. I told him, "I don't want to record this nightmare; I don't want to remember any of this."

I felt like I was watching a gripping movie with my hands over my eyes and I couldn't figure out what was happening in the story because I refused to look. I couldn't see God. I was so terrified, I didn't even know what to pray. My panic was leading to blindness. I was caught in a whirlwind. My fear of losing Noa was turning me into a bystander, a ghost hovering over my life.

That day I told myself: *If I can figure out a way to peel my hands off my eyes, there might be a great tale waiting for me. An action-packed epic filled with romance and suspense, fearless heroes, panoramic scenery, laughter, tears, hypnotic music. There will be fairies, of course, and magic, and timeless lessons to learn. And perhaps even a Hollywood ending. If I can only figure out how to peel my hands off my eyes and live with less fear.*

twenty-five

If you have nothing to lose, you can try everything.
YIDDISH PROVERB

I WAS sitting cross-legged on the floor trying to find a comfortable position to hold for the coming hour. I kept squirming. Ever since I got home from Jack's house, I had been determined to learn how to live with less fear. So here I was at a Buddhist meditation class in Santa Monica. It was the second Tuesday in December at noon. The teacher was a woman in her late forties dressed in white. She had a strong southern drawl; I'd been expecting an Indian guru. There were just three other students in the room—in other words, there was no way I could go unnoticed. I struggled to hold my position, closed my eyes, and expected to be lulled into a state of peace. I had studied meditation before. I had learned how to follow my breath and had practiced emptying my mind. I thought I knew what to expect.

The teacher said, "Today we're going to learn the death meditation." She said it was important to see that we could die at any moment. And she added, "Some of you who are young and healthy might be nodding your heads agreeing with me, but you're not really thinking you might die today." So the teacher decided to prove to us that we really *could* die that very day. She started listing all the ways we could die. We could die because a random air bubble got into our hearts. We could die from a sudden aneurysm. We could die in a crash coming home from the meditation class. We could die by choking on the lunch we would be eating after the meditation class.

My heart started racing. I had come looking for peace and this crazy woman was scaring me to death!

And just then I remembered the most powerful teaching I knew about overcoming fear, which came from Rabbi Nachman of Bratslav, a great Hasidic master who battled darkness and depression in his own personal life: "This whole world is a very narrow bridge, and the most important thing is to have no fear at all."

The idea was a big paradox. It began with brutal honesty: "This whole world is a very narrow bridge." Rabbi Nachman was saying that our challenge as humans is to recognize our frailty, to understand how brief our time here is. There is a rumbling beneath the surface of all things. We don't know what today will bring, what any day will bring. We live stunted lives by lying to ourselves that we are immortal. Rabbi Nachman was urging us to strip away that illusion, peer behind the curtain, and recognize that we're all going to die.

And then Rabbi Nachman insisted: "And the most important thing is to have no fear at all." Why not? If life's a narrow bridge, why shouldn't I fear? Why shouldn't I be petrified? I tried to imagine myself crossing a narrow rickety bridge above a great abyss and every step was fraught with peril. Of course I'd be terrified.

How could thinking about the narrow bridge melt one's fears? Because knowledge of the bridge can shut you down in fear and paralysis or it can open you up. If all I've got is this brief tenuous existence, I'd better live it to its fullest.

This teaching became my mantra when I was worrying over Noa and the death sentence that doctor had put on her. Rabbi Nachman wanted people to see that there is a death sentence hanging over all of us. There wasn't just a death sentence on Noa, there was a death sentence on everyone. There was a death sentence on me even as I sat stunted by my fear. What was I supposed to do? *All I can do is strive to live passionately and fearlessly for as long as I can.* In those moments when I was able to really take this teaching into my heart, my frozen limbs began to thaw out. I felt like the Tin Man in the *Wizard of Oz.* Rabbi Nachman's teaching was my oilcan. If I said it to myself at the right time, it gave me the power to bend and to move. With time, like the Tin Man, I might even learn to sing and to dance. I might even discover a heart beating inside my empty, bitter chest.

As I continued with my meditation class, I could feel the power of the death meditation working through me. I was becoming more aware of how little time I had left, and I felt a new courage to try things I had never tried before. As I practiced my death meditation each day and took in Rabbi Nachman's words, I was slowly starting to care much less about how people judged me. I was caring less about fitting in and striving to get accepted. There was just less time for that. I found myself caring more about doing what felt true. I looked in the mirror a lot less and tried to listen a lot more.

Embracing a death sentence was extraordinarily liberating. Small-level fears were beginning to seem inconsequential and irrelevant. I felt freer to take risks and to speak my mind. I was more open to change and to trying new things.

As I meditated I still had fears. But Rabbi Nachman's words

were giving me courage. There were times when my fear gave way to a calm I didn't even know existed inside me. It was a daily struggle to strive for that calm and that clarity. But even in those times when I felt more fear than calm, it brought me great comfort to know I was not alone in my fears.

I started to realize that we're all crossing that narrow bridge together, and it calmed me to hold on to the people around me. When you are on an airplane and there's turbulence, you suddenly find yourself connecting deeply with the stranger you had been ignoring for much of the flight. Suddenly you recognize that stranger as a trusted companion on a fragile, sacred journey. There are no strangers on a bumpy plane ride. I believed Rabbi Nachman wanted us to feel that richness, that honesty, that yearning for connection, that clinging to life every day. I believed he was asking me to feel deeply, to cast off self-delusion, to connect with people with an open heart and open hands.

This whole world is a very narrow bridge, and there was no time to waste. And the most important thing of all was to keep crossing the narrow bridge with courage and without fear.

As I continued meditating, I noticed I was remembering my dreams in great detail. I began keeping a dream journal at my bedside.

twenty-six

*A man's worst enemies can't wish on him what
he can think up himself.*

YIDDISH PROVERB

IT WAS the first night of Chanukah. Rob was making latkes, traditional potato pancakes fried in oil. The savory aroma was enough
to make me salivate. To surprise the kids I decided to create a menorah out of a banana. We played games, sang songs. We lit the banana
menorah. We gave Adi a Harry Potter book and Noa a Barbie doll.
The kids were in heaven. Noa was inching toward the menorah; I
could tell she was restraining herself. She so wanted to make a wish
and blow out the candles. I reminded her about the miracle of Chanukah, how there was only enough oil left in the ancient temple to
keep the light burning one day and how the light miraculously kept
shining for eight days and nights. She loved this story. She loved any
story where someone weak managed to get strong.

That night I dreamed I was trapped in a room and there were giant
monsters biting me. Giant horrible insects. It was scary and I was
terrified and I couldn't get the monsters off of me. I asked a man
passing by for help, but he was petrified and didn't help me.

101

The monsters kept biting at my flesh and growling and they were so scary-looking, with many legs and claws and sharp, pointy teeth.

Suddenly I had an idea. I took off my scarf and started dangling it in front of one monster until it bit the scarf and then I swung the monster around. Then another monster wanted a turn.

I hadn't dangled my scarf to create some sort of ride for them; my thought was to distract them or to possibly kill them. But they perceived it as a game, and I went along with it and played with them.

Suddenly, they were the sweetest puppies, begging for more, panting, lying on their backs waiting for a turn to ride on my scarf.

In the Talmud it says, "A dream that hasn't been interpreted is like a letter that hasn't been read." So here is what I wrote about this dream in my journal: *I often fear situations before I even come to know them. I blow things out of proportion. I turn challenges into nightmares, strangers into monsters. Sometimes I wait passively for help to come when I have the power to help myself.*

It was the moment in my dream when I decided to act that I was able to change the picture.

I believed this dream came to remind me to be creative, to think on my feet, and to act. It reminded me about the power of playfulness.

What was the power of playfulness? Fear can turn puppies into monsters. Playfulness can turn monsters into puppies. I certainly saw that in my own life. When I stood at a lectern preparing to speak before a huge crowd, I quickly learned how a little playful humor could turn a roomful of judgmental onlookers with their hands folded at their chests into a roomful of friends.

I knew I had a choice. I could see the unknown future with all my fears about Noa's health as a terrifying nightmare, or I could transform that nightmare into a thrilling ride. Perhaps I had the power to greet the future with hope and optimism and humor. Making a life with Rob, raising Adi and Noa *was* a thrilling ride, and too often I chose to dwell on the nightmare. It was Chanukah after all, a time for transforming darkness into light.

At the end of that journal entry I wrote: *If I have the choice between the monsters and the puppies, I want the puppies.*

twenty-seven

You lead me beside still waters. You restore my soul.

PSALM 23:2—3

WITH MY eyes closed I was flooded by the scent of the freshly cut grass wafting through the screen door. My mind was floating. I imagined I was in a pasture.

I was trying to meditate every day. I created a little sacred spot for myself in the corner of my study, which is a little hut in our backyard. I bought a tiny round green carpet about two feet in diameter and put a pillow on top of the carpet to sit on. It took a lot of effort for me to settle down in the mornings and meditate. It wasn't easy. I'm an antsy person.

When I was an antsy kid and couldn't sit still on the piano bench, I used to think my piano teacher was saying "Light, light." I wasn't sure what he meant. Should I turn on the light? Should I strike the piano keys more gently? It was many years later when I realized he was actually saying, "Alight." Alight, land, find yourself a resting place. In the biblical story when Noah wants to find out if the floodwaters have receded, he sends out the dove hoping she will fly away, but she returns to the ark because she can't alight. There's no place for her feet to rest.

In one of the worst biblical curses, God says to Israel: "You will find no resting place for your feet . . . Your life will be filled with doubt . . . In the morning you will say, 'If only it were night,' at night you will say, 'If only morning would come.'"

I thought about this restlessness, and I realized how it was mirrored in God. The Bible says that God wants to find a resting place in us. God wants a place to stay below. Every soul is a sanctuary for God. But if we are agitated and closed down, how can God alight? God holds the keys to many gates, God can unlock many doors. But there's one door God can't open and that's the door to the human heart. That's our job, to make a home for God within us.

When my soul was restless, when my mind was racing, when the road before me didn't just diverge but split into a million possible directions, I tried to alight.

Often before meditating I would fill a glass with cloudy tap water, set it down on the counter, and watch how clarity came. It calmed me like the Twenty-third Psalm: "You lead me beside still waters. You restore my soul . . . My cup runneth over."

Carving out a regular time to alight, I was beginning to open up to new hope.

I sat quietly in the corner of my study on the floor with the lights off. I still do it. I tend to be a bat. I prefer darkness to light, gray days to sunny ones, which is a bit of a challenge in LA. In the mornings I sat with my sunglasses on and the hood of my sweatshirt pulled over my head.

When a rabbi friend of mine saw me meditating in my hoodie and shades, she laughed. "You look like a celebrity in rehab." When

Rob peered in and saw me in my getup, he said he couldn't decide if I was a garden gnome or the Unabomber.

Day by day I sat and let the storm around me and within me subside. I let my muscles relax. I unclenched my jaw, my fist, my heart. I breathed deeply in and out. I imagined that each time I inhaled I was filling myself up with helium. I imagined I was getting lighter and lighter with each breath. I could feel myself rising up. And I imagined that each time I exhaled, I was letting go of everything that was weighing me down: anxiety, fear, worry, sadness, anger. I kept breathing in helium and breathing out heaviness.

I was beginning to notice that everything I was experiencing for the first time Noa already seemed to know. Because of her disability she did everything slowly. She walked slowly, played slowly, talked slowly, ate slowly. She understood people, she could read their faces, she could see the emotion behind the mask. One day she said to me, "Your friend Keith is a sad man." How did she know this? "How do you know this?" I asked. She said, "I don't know, every time I see him I see a sad man." Everyone who knew Keith saw a funny man, a successful man full of jokes and anecdotes. But Noa was right. Deep down he was a sad man.

With my eyes closed I saw Noa's power. I saw her wisdom. I saw her calm. Words from *Star Wars* flashed before me: "The force is strong with this one."

twenty-eight

I called out to God from my narrowness,
God answered me with a great expanse.

PSALM 118:5

Noa's second-grade teacher wasn't making eye contact with me. There we were, the two of us sitting alone on those little kiddy chairs in Noa's classroom. She was clearing her throat, trying to gather the courage to speak. She finally broke the silence; "Noa's behind." I didn't want to hear this.

Rob and I expended so much energy worrying over Noa's physical health and we comforted ourselves by thinking, "At least when she's sitting down in her classroom she'll be on an equal playing field." Noa was so wise, I was looking forward to watching her blossom at school. And now this woman was telling me she thought Noa had learning disabilities.

"I don't know how to teach her," Noa's teacher was telling me. But Noa loved her Jewish school, she loved going, she loved her friend Amanda. The two of them laughed and played in the school-yard every day. And Noa loved to pray. She loved getting to school every morning and singing Hebrew songs to God. I told the teacher,

"It will take time. Noa can catch up." The woman looked at me with pity; I looked away.

I knew it was taking me and Noa hours to do her homework after school every day. But with time and patience I decided she could catch up.

I looked straight into that pity glance coming my way and said, "She's only in second grade. Kids develop at different rates." I somehow convinced the teacher to be patient and keep an open mind about Noa.

With all my meditating I knew about letting go of all wants, but it took great effort to stop hoping for things to change.

Oh how I prayed for Noa to make huge leaps. She was "behind" physically and academically. The euphemism they used for Noa and for all the kids in the waiting room was "developmentally delayed." "Delayed" sounds like something temporary and doable. All you have to do is hurry up and work harder and you can catch up.

I remembered when I was growing up there was a kid in my class who was taking high-school math in the third grade. He was so far ahead of the rest of us schmoes. And then I met up with him as an adult and he was just a schmoe like all the rest of us—he didn't discover the cure for cancer or build on Einstein's theory of relativity. He was a very bright working stiff, holding down a job and raising a family.

Doesn't it all even out in the end?

And then I thought about my own life and my own professional hiatus. How was I ever going to catch up? After all, I'd spent the past few years falling.

I thought about all the pressure we put on ourselves to keep up in some imaginary race. My neighbor's son was in high school staying up till all hours of the night studying for AP this and honors that.

I thought about Adi and the crazy thing that had happened to him on the way to kindergarten. Adi had already been accepted into two kindergartens, and then in the last week of preschool his teacher sat us down and said, "I'm not sure Adi is ready for kindergarten." When I asked why she said, "When it's time for journal writing, Adi just scribbles and the other kids write. And whenever we do table work Adi doesn't want to sit down." I was flabbergasted. The two kindergartens that had already accepted him didn't seem to worry about his scribbles.

Later that very afternoon I was taking a close look at Adi, trying to see him as objectively as any mother can see her child. And I noticed that his eyes were ever so slightly crossed. The next day I took him to an ophthalmologist. The doctor examined Adi and said it was fortunate I had noticed this problem. It turned out that Adi was extremely farsighted and practically blind in his left eye. We'd need to get him into glasses immediately and patch his stronger eye six hours per day. I told the doctor about what his preschool teacher had said about Adi not being ready for kindergarten. He said to me, "Of course your kid isn't doing work at the table, he can't SEE anything up close. Put him in glasses and take him to kindergarten."

Yes, with glasses Adi magically caught up. But was life about catching up? Was it a race?

I started studying Jewish mystical texts with Toba about contracted thinking and expansive thinking. I learned that when we are in a state of contraction, we suffer from linear thinking. We get easily shaken, caught in the details; we lose sight of the bigger picture. When we are in a state of expansive thinking, we can see how everything fits together into a larger scheme. Suddenly everything makes sense— our true purpose, our connection to something so much larger than ourselves, our connection to one another and to all of creation.

This teaching resonated very deeply for me. I mapped it out.

According to this teaching there were two ways to look at life. The first way was to see life as a race. If you view life as a race, then you will always be in a competition. Your objective is to win. People who need your help are an annoyance, they are slowing you down. Living in a competitive environment takes a toll on the body and the soul. The adrenaline rush inevitably gives way to exhaustion. Frustration sets in, anger sets in, tunnel vision sets in. It's hard to notice all the beauty that surrounds you when your eyes are fixed in only one direction. Who has time to rest? If you rest you might lose precious ground. The race tends to nurture black-and-white thinking— you're either in or you're out. To combat uncertainty rigidity sets in, routine sets in. Creativity suffers. How can you make time for fun when you suspect your colleagues are busy at work? When life is a race, you're always trying to catch up. There's always someone ahead of you. Can you be happy if you can't win?

Then I thought of that Aesop's fable about the tortoise and the hare. *It may be a source of good wisdom about tenacity (slow and steady wins the race),* I thought, *but it's a really sad way to live your life.* Even though the tortoise won the race, he was still alone. He was alone the whole long time he was competing, locked in his own hard, dry shell. I continued thinking . . . *Life as a race is so predictably linear, there's no time for stops along the way, no time for meandering and taking circuitous paths. Where's the beauty in it, where's the adventure in it, where's the joy in it? Instead you find yourself uttering the defeatist mantra: Let me just get through the day.* I was sick of repeating that mantra.

But if contracted thinking was like living in a race, then expansive thinking was like living inside a Hora, a circle folk dance. I asked myself, *What if instead of seeing life as a race, we could begin to see life as a Hora?* That's what the teaching was saying. If life is a circle dance, your objective is to participate. It's not about beating others, it's about joining in. If life is a dance, you begin to see yourself as part of a community. Life as a dance has no beginning and no end, no winners and no losers. It has a sound track, it involves music and steps and improvisation. Life as a dance is fun, exhilarating. It nurtures a sense of ease, it encourages flexibility, inventiveness. Routine gives way to surprise, to new ways of thinking. Your eyes take in the world around you. The chaotic, breathtaking whirl of it all. When you are tired, you can take a break with the knowledge that you can always join in again. If you need help, you can lean on the people to your right and to your left. You can place your hands on their shoulders and let them hold you up. You begin to see yourself as part of an invisible web of connection uniting all people. Life as a dance is a sacred act. You're not here to *get through* the day; you're here to *improve* the day. To see something new, do something new, give something new.

I thought to myself, *The question a person in a race asks is: How far ahead am I? The question a person in a dance asks is: How wide is my circle?*

That day I told myself: *It's not a race. You don't need to catch up. You need to open up. Open yourself up and inspiration will come, creativity will come. Answers will come. New ways of approaching old problems will come. Open yourself up and you will see your way of entering the world.*

And of course I thought about Noa. She wasn't in a race. My job as her mother was to help her discover her voice, her light, her way.

My thinking was expanding. Day by day I was leaving my small angry dark thoughts behind and opening myself up to new ways of experiencing reality.

And Noa was making incremental steps. I could see them now. She had more stamina, she was teetering less. She was growing in her own beautiful way, on her own trajectory.

twenty-nine

The woods would be very silent if no birds sang except the best.

YIDDISH PROVERB

I WAS sitting at my desk writing notes, pages and pages of questions about our ability to detect the openings that appear in our lives. With all my hopes about expansive thinking and living in a Hora, I realized I still needed to figure out how to enter the circle. I'd reached a roadblock in my writing, and I decided to go into my bedroom.

And there was a little bird sitting on my bed.

The bird saw me, got scared, and flew right into the glass window—and knocked itself out. It woke up, and flew right back into the window and fell down again. It got up and started flying around the room. I kept running after it, and I found myself talking to it, "Birdie, don't do it. The window is closed."

Then it perched itself right on my nightstand, right on top of my notes about finding an opening in our lives. As it sat there, I opened the glass door in our bedroom and the bird flew out. I went to my nightstand and saw that the bird had relieved itself all over my notes. The droppings had leaked through all five pages of my notes.

I thought it was a sign.

I realized you can have all the equipment to soar, you can have wings to fly, but if you can't see properly, you're going to smash your head against a window. It isn't enough to be able to picture the world beyond you; the challenge is to find your unique opening, your way to get there.

I knew I wasn't alone. I understood that most people have that experience sometime in their lives. They can picture their path perfectly, they can see where they want to go, but they keep coming up against a wall.

Watching Noa, I could see there were so many obstacles in her path, physical limitations, learning disabilities, but she was very good at opening doors. It seemed as if she had been given the perfect personality for her disabilities. She was blessed with patience, courage, and optimism. She would fall and hurt herself and just pop back up and try again. Children are easily frustrated when they can't do something perfectly or easily. They end up crumpling up their own artwork or smashing whatever they are building. But Noa always had unlimited patience for completing a task. She would sit there for hours just trying to cut out a single picture. And that combination of patience, courage, and optimism gave Noa the keys to so many doors that would have otherwise been locked to her.

Noa's mother, on the other hand, kept smashing her head against the wall. I could see that. That bird in my bedroom seemed to be telling me, "Stop and take a careful look at your situation. When your vision expands, you will suddenly see choices, alternate routes."

I thought to myself, *If you just keep hitting your head against the wall, you're going to give yourself a concussion. Step back, look around, examine your options.*

Why was that wall there? Why wasn't I moving forward in my life?

Was I a victim? Had I built the wall with my own hands? Had I been too shy or too proud or too scared to ask for help? Had I fallen into a state of resignation or despair?

Maybe I needed to locate a new path, *my* path, *my* opening.

There are moments in life when a light suddenly appears. In my case it was a little bird with a bad headache. It was a moment of pure clarity. I would seek out help, I would go to a therapist, I would make peace with God, I would expand my circle, lean on my friends. I would learn how to tell the difference between a closed window and an open door.

A bird sat on my bed, left its droppings all over over my notes, and sang this teaching to me.

thirty

If God wants people to suffer, He sends them
too much understanding.
YIDDISH PROVERB

THERE WAS one more place where Rob and I just kept smashing
our heads up against a wall. We both wanted to have another
baby. We'd planned Noa's birth with such hubris, never thinking
anything could go wrong. Now we fretted over a possible future
child, thinking everything could go wrong. We had always planned
on having four kids, but the doctors couldn't tell us what Noa had and
they couldn't promise us the next child would be healthy. I envied the
religious moms in the waiting room. The Orthodox Jewish mothers
and the Evangelical Christian mothers I spoke with had something in
common—intense faith that propelled them forward. I knew mothers in the waiting room who had children with genetic disorders and
who got pregnant again without even thinking about having an am-
niocentesis. They saw the trajectory of their lives as the unfolding of
God's plan. And their unquestioning faith allowed them to push forward into the uncertain future with the belief that God was on their
side.

I didn't have that kind of faith. I wasn't sure whose side God was on. Or if God was on any side.

Every night Rob and I would replay the same conversation. I'd say, "Yes, I've decided, let's have a baby." And he'd say, "No, I don't think we should." And the next night Rob would start the conversation, "I've changed my mind, I'm ready to have another child." And I'd say, "No, I'm too scared to do it." And that's how we'd go back and forth night after night.

We just couldn't make a decision to move forward. We couldn't let go of the wish to have another child and yet we were too frightened to actually go through with it. Noa's neurologist told us we had a 25 percent chance of having another child like Noa. But we didn't know what "like Noa" meant. Was her condition static or was it a rare fatal degenerative disease? No one knew for sure.

I wanted to make a decision about whether to have another child or not. I didn't want to just keep going back and forth in a never-ending seesaw with Rob. And I didn't want to let nature make the decision for me.

My great-aunt Sophie (no relation to the dog) married in her early thirties, which was quite late for a Jewish woman born and raised in a small village in Poland. When she and her husband, Herschel, first married, they shunned the idea of having children. They were now highly educated New York intellectuals. *The world is overpopulated*, they insisted. But when Sophie entered her forties, she began to regret her decision. More than anything, she longed to have a child to raise and cherish. One night Sophie came to visit my grandmother Rachel (my mother's mother) and whispered her secret: "I missed my period. I think I might be pregnant!" My grandmother forced a smile and hoped with her. When Sophie left the apartment, my grandmother turned to my mother with sadness in her eyes and said, "I think it's menopause." Indeed, my grandmother's suspicion was correct.

My mother told me this story long ago, and its poignancy has always remained with me.

No matter what the Rolling Stones say, time isn't on our side. It cheats us, robs us, frustrates us. Time is indifferent—even to the Rolling Stones.

I knew this fact all too well, but I just couldn't make a clear and final decision. Rob and I kept trading places. Why didn't I have the kind of perfect faith that would enable me to take the leap? I wanted blind faith. But how do you put out your own eyes?

The God Who Sees Me

tHIRty-oNe

If God were living on earth, people would break His windows.

YIDDISH PROVERB

EVER SINCE Noa's second-grade teacher approached me, my mood had taken a nosedive. Why was Noa having so much trouble learning? Why?

It was only 5:00 p.m., but it was dark outside. The room was stuffy and overheated. I was sitting in a therapist's giant leather chair feeling small and nervous, not knowing what to expect or what to say. His name was Dr. Bittman. He was a big man, lumbering, with droopy eyes, and his office was dusty and the furniture was heavy.

Dr. Bittman was slouched in his worn leather chair; from where I was sitting I could hear his stomach growling. Finally, he looked at me and spoke up, "Ms. Levy, what brings you here?" I got very emotional, and I wanted to talk about God. I asked him, "Where is God?" I said I'd been praying for an answer. I started tearing up, and I looked over . . . and he was sleeping. My therapist was out cold.

I woke him up. I said, "HELLO!" And his whole body jerked the way it does when you wake up suddenly. "You were sleeping," I said. And he said, "No I wasn't."

"Yes you were."

"No I wasn't."

"I woke you; your whole body jerked."

"I wasn't sleeping," he insisted.

It got really quiet in the room except for his stomach, and then he looked at me and said, "Well, hypothetically, if I *were* sleeping, how would that make you *feel?*"

I thought to myself, *I can't even hold a therapist's attention, how can I expect to hold God's attention?*

I was a rabbi and God was no comfort to me.

Who was my God? I thought about the way God appeared in the Bible through so many different lenses. Every biblical personality encountered God in a very personal and specific way. Abraham's God was an aloof, even sadistic, God of tests, who was willing to pit morality, love, and compassion against faith. Jacob's approach to God was all about Monty Hall and *Let's Make a Deal*—"If you do this for me, I'll do that for you." Moses' God was all Hollywood, a God of special effects and pyrotechnics—ten plagues, seas parting.

On the High Holy Days, I was taught to see a God who was punishing and judgmental. A God who sits on a throne evaluating all our deeds and decides who will live and who will die.

Who was my God?

There certainly were times in my life when I hated God. Times when I could not pray. Times when I could not even bring myself to say Kaddish, the Jewish memorial prayer, for my own father, who taught me to love God, who taught me how to pray, who brought me to synagogue every Sabbath and let me hide beneath the wings of his prayer shawl.

There were times in my life when I couldn't say Kaddish for my own father because the Kaddish praises God, and I had no words of praise inside me for a deaf God. For a God who did not prevent my sweet father's murder.

Then years later, when I was in my freshman year of college, I was walking on campus with an umbrella one rainy spring day. Everyone was carrying an umbrella. And a simple question popped into my head. Did I actually think God was my personal umbrella? My shelter? Was God going to keep me safe and dry? It suddenly seemed strange to me the way people would say, "God's watching over me" when innocent children were dying all over the world every day. Shouldn't God be watching over them too? I began to see that it was my faith in the Superman God that had caused me to hate God. My belief in a God who swooped down to protect good people from pain and to punish wicked people for their sins made me doubt God's existence. It wasn't true. God wasn't anyone's personal bodyguard.

One day at the end of that year I said to myself, "It's time to bury the vision of the old man. It's time for the network to cancel Superman, he's had a good long run, but it's time for him to go."

It wasn't easy to let go of the picture of God from the children's Bible my father used to read to me. I loved that old man with the flowing white beard looking down on me almost as much as I loved my father. I missed Him. I wanted to say Kaddish for Him. A grand Kaddish for the mighty God who once inhabited the great dreams of my youth.

So if God wasn't Superman, who *was* God?

My worries over Noa's physical health were now compounded by my worries over her cognitive health. Even though I was meditating, even though I was less fearful, even though I knew I had so many blessings, I still felt like I was floating above my life. For two years I had scheduled my days around Noa's therapies and doctors' appointments. Now there were new appointments to face—Noa needed to be assessed by learning specialists and neuropsychologists.

One day in February, I was sitting in a café sipping coffee when these words suddenly popped into my head: "Where are you coming from and where are you going?" I kept repeating these words over and over again to myself. I knew these words. An angel spoke them to a slave lost in the desert. But as I sat there with my coffee, a mother lost in her worry, I was sure these words were summoning me.

When I got home I opened the Bible and began poring over the ancient story. I'd known the story of this lost slave named Hagar all my life, but I'd always glossed over her because she seemed to be a relatively unimportant character in the Bible. I had never tried to see the world through her eyes before. On that day I began reading her story with new eyes. There she was standing before me. So strong and dignified. I envisioned her, this young beauty with smooth olive skin, thick black wavy hair, deep brown eyes, and callused hands from a life of hard labor. It was she who taught me how to see God.

In the Bible, Hagar was a slave to Abram and Sarai. Sarai was infertile, so Abram slept with Hagar in order to have a child through her. Sarai grew jealous when Hagar conceived and began to torment her. And Hagar ran away.

As she was wandering alone in the wilderness, an angel of God found her. The angel asked her, "Where are you coming from and where are you going?" Hagar told him she was running away from her mistress Sarai. The angel promised Hagar she was going to be the matriarch of a great people. He told her to go back to Sarai and assured her that the child she was carrying would grow up to be a leader of men. The angel instructed her to name the baby Ishmael—which means "God will hear"—because God had heard her suffering.

Hagar took in the angel's prophecy and she said to God, "You are El Roi; You are The God Who Sees Me." Others looked at Hagar and saw a slave. God saw a matriarch.

Hagar did go back to Abram, and she had a child. A beautiful boy named Ishmael, God will hear.

What a relief to finally be seen. I understood that God didn't do a thing for Hagar except to remind her of her own power. And that's why a lonely, lost slave gave God a new name: The God Who Sees Us as we are and reminds us of who we can be.

I couldn't pray to Rob's Just In Case, the God of candles on birthday cakes. I wanted more than a wish and a breath. But Hagar's El Roi spoke to my soul. *God sees me, God is listening.*

I walked out to my backyard, sat on the grass, and whispered to Hagar's God, "Can You see my Noa? What do You see? Is there a beautiful future awaiting her? Can You see her strength? Her wisdom? Her greatness? I won't ask You to fix her, but I'm pleading with You, teach me to see hope for her future. Tell me about the rabbits, George." Tears streamed down my face. I continued, "And what do You make of me? Do You see how lost I am? What do You see that I can't see?"

I was quiet for some time and then a sensation of warmth began traveling through my body. I don't have words for this feeling except to say I suddenly felt un-alone. An overwhelming sense of fullness.

A calm descended upon my chest; I could feel its heat in my breath. A palpable Presence seemed to be telling me, "I am with you." And I broke down and wept tears of gratitude.

I lay down in the grass with my arms spread wide, staring at the blue sky. In my times of great fear and worry I had pushed God away. When Noa dreamed about God being near her, I imagined that God wanted to take her from me. That's why I told God to stay away from her. But now I understood that God never left me or Noa or anyone else. God was with us all along. Noa knew this instinctively. It took her mother the rabbi a bit more time to figure it out. God wasn't a body snatcher looking for the right moment to steal our loved ones away from us. And God wasn't a cruel judge looking for ways to catch us and punish us. God wasn't Superman ready to swoop down and protect us from all harm, and God wasn't Santa Claus reading our minds and giving us whatever we prayed for.

I understood that even with God, life wasn't necessarily going to be a picnic.

El Roi made some promises to Hagar, but not promises that it was all going to be perfect. Her son was going to give her heartache. God told her things would get better, and they would also get worse. *Yes,* I thought, *life is a blessing and it's also a curse. No one's got it easy, no one's immune to suffering, no matter how good we are.*

Later that night I wrote down these thoughts to myself in my journal: *God believes in Noa. God believes in all people. And God is praying we will come to see in ourselves what God already sees. God is hoping we will live out the life that's lying within us.*

God is trying to make eye contact with us. The God Who Sees Me is calling, "Where are you coming from and where are you going?"

We don't have much time. The Psalm says, "Our days on earth are like a shadow." One commentary on this verse asks, "What sort of shadow?" The answer offered is, "Not as the shadow cast by a wall, or as the shadow cast by a tree, but as the shadow cast by a bird flying overhead."

So, I asked myself, *what are you waiting for?*

thirty-two

*Open my lips God, and let my mouth speak
Your praise.*

DAILY JEWISH PRAYER

I T WAS a Sunday morning. Noa was sitting on her pink bicycle with training wheels we'd bought her two years before. Rob had been trying to teach Noa how to push the pedals for months. We'd both been looking mournfully at the bike lately and wondering if we shouldn't just give it away to a child who might get some use out of it.

When parents raise a typical child, the early milestones of childhood are marked with excitement and picture taking, but soon they begin to take the progress for granted. They assume that once their child walks, he or she will eventually begin to skip and run and jump. But when you have a child with disabilities, even the slightest improvement takes on enormous proportions.

Noa was perched on her bike on the sidewalk in front of our house and I was cheering her on, "Push!" Nothing was happening. Rob started walking alongside the bike with his hands on the handlebars, giving Noa a ride. He walked her back to the strip of sidewalk in front of our house and glanced up at me with a look of defeat. Suddenly,

Noa somehow got her feet to work in harmony. There was a slight push and then another. I took a deep breath in and suddenly for the first time in a very long time there was a spontaneous prayer on my lips: "Thank you, God. May her strength continue to increase before us each day."

To pray again. To pray with passion, with feeling. To speak freely with an open heart. My parched soul was overflowing.

I wasn't thanking God for curing Noa. I was thanking God for the ability to see. Thanking God for the ability to treasure the incremental steps even though there was a long road ahead of us.

Watching Noa make tiny but monumental steps forward taught me how to pray again. She taught me to see the unnoticed miracles, the daily blessings. And I was so grateful. Grateful for each morning, for every improvement, for the gift of life. Of course, I was still worried. And sometimes I was mournful for all the effort it took Noa to achieve skills that came as simple reflexes to other children. Sometimes I was angry. Why should any child face such struggle? Sometimes I was impatient. I longed for dramatic improvement even though I knew my child would blossom in her own way and in her own time.

But through it all I now kept trying to talk to God.

I've always loved the Yiddish saying "From your mouth to God's ear." It's a phrase I was taught to say whenever someone wishes you well. Your friend says, "I hope you get that job." And you respond, "From your mouth to God's ear."

The saying is full of chutzpah. It implies that the God of the universe might actually care about you and me. And yet, there's a mournfulness embedded inside the saying itself. If only God could hear all that we long for. If only God *could* grant all our wishes. If only. This hopeful proverb tinged with sadness already understands that there might be a very long distance between your mouth and God's ear.

But I was starting to believe "your mouth" and "God's ear" were much closer than I had ever imagined. I was starting to believe in a God who listened, who heard, who cared. Who was just as outraged as we were by life's unfairness, just as pained. A God who was not distant and unfeeling, but compassionate. A God who suffered when we suffered.

I started to believe that God was listening, and that God was answering us too. Now I could see that God's answer to my prayers was quite different from the answer I'd been searching for. No, God wasn't going to get anyone the job they'd been praying for or stop a war or prevent a natural disaster. God's reply came as the strength to fight on, the courage to face what I was fearing. God's answer was the ability to accept what I had been denying. God's answer appeared to me as hope in the face of despair. When I stopped waiting for miracles and started opening up my soul to God, my prayers suddenly started working. I could pray for strength and receive strength. That's something Noa understood instinctively. God was her anchor, the Rock who grounded her. She knew how to pray for balance and receive balance.

I was now coming to see prayer as an experience, not a request. It was a sense of being connected, of being part of something larger than myself. It was an attempt to be in the presence of God.

I no longer looked to God to prevent life's ugliness or to cure it. I was looking to God to show me how to prevent the cruelty I had the power to prevent. I no longer saw God as a force that could shield me or anyone else from harm, but as a presence who had the power to point us all toward the holiness that resides in simple acts.

Once I stopped blaming God for everything that went wrong, I could stop hating God and start listening to God.

I was listening. But part of me was still hoping that God would make my decisions for me and tell me exactly what to do.

tHiRty-tHRee

No choice is also a choice.

YIDDISH PROVERB

I WAS hunched over my dining room table scribbling out a list of pros and cons: Should we take Noa out of her school and put her in a school for kids with learning disabilities? Should we leave her in her current school and give it more time? Would she be crushed to leave her school? Was it a mistake to take her out of her Jewish school and put her in a secular school? Were we hurting her by keeping her in a school that wasn't equipped for her? Should I try to homeschool her?

Perhaps El Roi was with me, but El Roi wasn't going to make any decisions for me. That was my job. I'd repeat the Yiddish proverb to myself, "You can't sit on two horses with one behind." I wanted to have it both ways. I couldn't decide whether to have another baby or not. I couldn't decide if it was time to reenter professional rabbinic life or not. Even if I were to resume my professional life, I couldn't decide what path to take. Should I teach in a school? Should I seek out a congregation? Should I write? Even if I chose to write, I couldn't decide what to write.

The truth is, I've never been good at making decisions. I have trouble deciding what shampoo to buy. Sometimes in the supermarket I stand there frozen in the shampoo aisle just reading all the different labels: *this one makes your hair shiny and that one gives it volume and the next one tames the frizz* . . . At our wedding my brother Danny gave a toast and said my decision to marry Rob was the only decision he had ever seen me make with confidence. That's true. I married Rob without ever making a single list of pros and cons.

I thought there were two ways to approach every decision. There are times when the best approach is to wait it out until the clouds part. You tell yourself, just be patient and it will all work itself out. And there are other times that require us to make a choice and push forward. When the Children of Israel were escaping from Egypt, they came upon the Red Sea and then they looked behind them and saw the Egyptians approaching. They were trapped. They cried to Moses, so he cried to God. And God shot back, "Why are you crying to Me? Tell the people to start walking." It was only after the people walked into the water that the sea parted before them.

Sometimes we need to be patient and answers will come. And sometimes we need to act and miracles will come. The only problem is, how do you know which time you're in? One of the hardest questions to answer in life is: *Does the situation I'm in require patience or action?* Even Moses, whom the Bible describes as the greatest prophet who ever lived, couldn't tell. He prayed at the Red Sea and God told him, "Stop praying, start walking." And he hit the rock when he should have been patient.

Was it wrong to be patient when Noa needed academic interventions? Or was removing her from a school she loved a rash and impetuous move?

I kept asking myself, "How do you get past confusion and insecurity?" Doubt is such a huge impediment. It's the root of so much paralysis. Not knowing which way to turn or what to do.

To confuse matters further, I was studying with Toba one morning and we read a commentary that said we have two choices every time we have to make a decision. The first is to act with conviction by exercising our God-given power of free choice. The second is to do nothing and leave it to chance. According to this approach, the way of patience was the way of passivity.

I knew this all too well. Sometimes we mistakenly fool ourselves into believing that leaving a situation to chance is leaving it to God. We say to ourselves, "It's in God's hands" or "Let go and let God," or we look for clues from above and say to ourselves, "It's a sign." But now I was beginning to see that to leave things to chance is to deny the power of God working in us. It is to deny our own divine image. We want to leave it in God's hands and remain confused and do nothing. But God wants us to put it back in *our* hands and make a choice between this road and that one.

One of my favorite rabbinic proverbs is, "There is no joy greater than the resolution of doubt." Yes, clarity is pure bliss, but how do you get to that bliss?

How would I know the right path to take? Making decisions was never my strong suit. I wished I just knew the right answer. I wished I could see how the story would end for me and for Noa.

And then one night I sprang up in bed, turned on my lamp, and wrote in my journal.

What if . . .

What if by some miracle the heavens were to open and God called out to you and made the decision for you? What if God told you exactly what to do? How would you feel? Swayed? Relieved? Disturbed? Oppositional?

I realized I would feel oppositional!

I was always jealous when I read the biblical tales about the Children of Israel in the desert, because there in the wilderness, God made all their decisions for them. They didn't have to fret over choices. They didn't have to make lists of pros and cons. They didn't have to flip a coin. They didn't have to seek the advice of a parent or a friend or a mentor or a therapist, and they didn't have to search their souls either. They didn't even have to pray to God for an answer.

The Bible tells us the Israelites had a portable holy tent of God that they took with them on all their travels. By day, God appeared to them as a cloud; by night, as a pillar of fire. Wherever the cloud went, they followed. Wherever the pillar of fire led them, they walked on as God lit up the night. Whenever the cloud stopped and settled upon the tent, the people would make camp. They remained there as long as the cloud hovered over the tent no matter how many days it rested there. When the cloud lifted off the tent, they set out on their journey. "By the command of God they camped and by the command of God they journeyed on."

How did the Children of Israel feel about being told what to do? They wept. They rebelled. They started to romanticize slavery in Egypt. God told them exactly where to go, but they wanted to carve out their own path. God wanted to speak to the people directly at Mount Sinai, but it was all too intense for them, too much, they didn't want to get that close to God. So they backed off. They said to Moses, "You listen to God and then you can share whatever you've learned with us."

I asked myself: *Were they evil? Wrong? Even Moses told God to back off. He said, "Leave me alone, lay off, I can't do it anymore. Kill me right now, God."*

And then I began to see that there is a deep human need to

rebel against predetermined answers and prearranged plans. It's hard to appreciate things we don't have to work for and discover on our own. Being told what to do leaves us feeling empty. Human beings have a need to struggle, to toil, to think, and to choose.

I understood this; being given all the answers can deplete us, even when they are the right answers.

The forty years in the desert were a time of learning. A band of slaves brought low learned to stand tall. They learned to treasure freedom so much that they were even willing to push God away so that they might exercise that freedom.

And the journey through the wilderness was a time of learning for God as well. The God who intervened in history with a mighty hand and an outstretched arm learned to practice the art of subtlety, "And I shall hide my face from you."

Seeing God can crush us,.seeking God can lift us up.

And that's when I gave myself a pep talk: *Nomi, I think you can be pretty certain that the heavens are not going to open up anytime soon, God is not going to call out to you and make your decision for you. God is never going to tell you exactly what to do.*

Instead of viewing this time of uncertainty as a tragedy, embrace it as a gift from above. Your freedom is a holy blessing. Your power to choose is a miracle.

For heaven's sake, stop wavering, stop procrastinating, stop waiting for miracles. The greatest miracle is lying dormant inside you right now. Make a decision. Sweat over it. Toil over it. Weigh all your options. Get sage advice. Make lists. Trust your gut, trust your instincts. Search your soul. Pray to God. But don't pray like a helpless slave waiting to be told what to do. Pray like a free person searching for strength and wisdom and insight.

Choose a path. Stay with your path. Be ready to face obstacles blocking your way. Even if you take a wrong turn, at least it will be your turn. Your life, your mistake. You will have learned which road not to take in the future. And besides, you will be moving. Your spiritual coma will be lifting. Your legs won't be asleep anymore. Your muscles will grow stronger. You will meet wonderful people and see breathtaking sights.

So my uncertainty wasn't a tragedy, it was a gift. Maybe there was a way to take a leap forward.

That very week my friend Shari phoned to tell me about the huge leap she'd made. Shari was elated and she asked me to perform her wedding ceremony. I was overjoyed. I hadn't performed a single marriage since the night of Dr. Becket's call more than two years earlier, and now I could see something was already shifting inside me. I was ready to step forward as her friend and her rabbi.

I repeated to myself the words I had written in my journal: *You will be moving. Your spiritual coma will be lifting.*

Okay, I thought to myself, *but when?*

thirty-four

And it shall come to pass on that day, that the mountains shall drip sweet wine, and the hills shall flow with milk.

JOEL 4:18

O N A beautiful sunny day on a terrace overlooking San Francisco Bay, I had the honor of marrying Shari and Yonatan. They had already tied the knot in Israel; this was their American wedding. Their son Nadiv was running between their legs making quite a racket. Finally Shari picked him up and held him tight. He listened intently as his parents entered a covenant of love and marriage.

Shari and I lived together in college. We quickly became close friends and would stay up late at night sharing our dreams for the future. Dreams of true love and marriage and kids. We dreamed about being full and worried about feeling empty. After graduation Shari became a lawyer and moved to Israel. When she was thirty she told herself, "If I'm not married by thirty-five, I'm going to have a kid by myself." She didn't want to wait for a man until she was too old to have a child. She dated here and there, but didn't find the right person to share her life with. So she made a decision to have a child alone.

She found a steady job, rented a home, and still hoped to find her soul mate. She found herself hoping for the man and planning for the child.

Why did Shari want a child? Motherhood was a life experience she didn't want to miss out on. She wanted to be pregnant, to experience the miracle of childbirth. She wanted to raise a child, to experience the kind of love that only exists between a parent and a child. She had so much love inside her heart to give. She knew that without a child she would feel empty.

Shari understood that having a child is one of those decisions that is irreversible. You can get married and divorced, you can take a job and quit a job, buy a home and sell a home. But a child would be forever.

Yes, Shari had fears. She worried that she would be a horrible mom. She feared she would lose patience. She worried that something might happen to her—as a single mom she'd have no backup. She was scared to get sick. She worried about how her child might judge her or be resentful for being brought into this world without a father. Shari had no idea what to expect. What would the baby be like? Who would she be as a mom? But there was one thing she did not fear: what the neighbors might say.

At thirty-seven she decided to have a child through artificial insemination. When Shari found out she was pregnant she was ecstatic, elated. And all her questions and fears resurfaced as well. *How will I take care of my child? What will I name it? Will I be able to do this?* Now it was real. But between the moments of fear, there was such excitement and expectation.

Giving birth was an incredible relief. Shari saw her son and experienced a bliss she had never known before. This baby, this new human being, came out of her and he was so beautiful. She named him Nadiv, which means "generous."

And still there was fear. He was so tiny. She didn't know how to change a diaper. She didn't know how to nurse him. She was afraid to take him home from the hospital to an empty house. She was overwhelmed by the enormity of the responsibility she would have to face alone. Being a single parent would be difficult. She'd never have a break. She started to cry. *I can't believe that I actually did this. My life will change so drastically and I'm here doing this by myself.*

Luckily, Shari had lots of friends, a terrific community of people who were there for her. It was a network of true support.

When I asked Shari how she gathered the strength to live out of order, to have the baby before the husband, she told me that having a biological clock helped her make her decision. The fact that she could no longer wait for chapter 1 to fall into place was a strong impetus for her to skip straight to chapter 2. She said, "Life is too short to wait for chapter 1 if you really want chapter 2."

There was one more worry Shari had after her son was born. She worried that having the kid would make it harder to find the guy.

Ironically, that's what attracted Yonatan to Shari. He was intrigued that she had a child on her own, that she was strong and independent. Yonatan was a pediatrician. He loved children. His wife had died several months before and now he was ready to live again. He signed on to a computer dating service hoping to meet his soul mate. One profile caught his eye. It was a picture of a beautiful woman with bright green eyes and curly blond hair with a baby in a backpack. Along with the photo was this description:

> I'm Shari. I'm a 39-year-old female . . . I'm single (never married) and I have 1 kid who lives with me always. I'm interested in a long-term relationship or marriage . . . I'm sensitive,

intelligent, determined, and strong willed. A person who loves
the outdoors and loves to laugh . . . I chose to have a child on
my own because I didn't want to miss this opportunity. My son
is 20 months old and the most amazing person. Of course, he
doesn't, can't, and shouldn't meet all my needs and I would still
really like to have a special person in my life . . . The person
I'm looking for can communicate, is easygoing and secure with
himself. Intelligent and self-motivated. Someone who shares
my values about life and the world. Good and loving with
children . . .

Shari and Yonatan decided to meet at a park. He was kind and calm
and thoughtful and smart. He had brought a gift for Nadiv. It all un-
folded so naturally. Love. Life. Nadiv fell in love with Yonatan too.

One day as she was driving Nadiv home from school, Shari
said, "Maybe we'll start calling Yonatan Daddy." Nadiv replied, "But
Mommy, he's *my* daddy, not yours."

Yes, Yonatan was attracted to the fact that Shari was a single
mother. Here was a woman who made a decision on her own to have a
child. Here was a strong, determined person who was going to get what
she wanted. And because there was no ex-husband in the picture,
Yonatan wouldn't be competing with someone or replacing someone
in the role of father.

Shari reminded me: "Doing step 2 helped me get step 1."

They were married in Israel under a tent in the hills of Galilee.
They could see goats and sheep grazing in the distance. It was a peaceful, calm day. Surrounded by friends, they stood beneath the wedding
canopy. Nadiv was in Shari's arms through the entire ceremony.
Yonatan recited the traditional Jewish formula of marriage to Shari:

"Behold you are betrothed to me as my wife according to the Law of Moses and the People of Israel." Then he turned to Nadiv and said, "Behold you are my son." And everyone wept.

Not long after their wedding, Yonatan was admitted into a post-doctoral fellowship at Johns Hopkins University. They moved to the United States and soon Shari became pregnant and they had a son together. They named him Matan, "a gift." It was a very different experience for Shari. Now there was someone with her through the whole pregnancy, through the birth and through life. And yes, now she would need to compromise with someone on all the decisions she used to make on her own.

One day I was talking to Shari on the phone. She was the director of a nonprofit foundation and she also sat on the board of directors of her kids' school. She was trying to tell me, "Life is too short to wait for things to happen. You have to make things happen." It was hard for her to finish her thought; there was too much going on around her. In the background I could hear her two boys trying to get her attention, "Mommy, hang up already." Yonatan accidentally picked up the extension as we spoke. So many distractions.

At that moment I remembered the dreams we'd shared in college and I said to myself, "Shari is full."

When I thought of Shari, I told myself: *A biological clock isn't only ticking for women in their late thirties. We're all here on a temporary visa.* The lesson was simple enough: If chapter 1 is missing, skip to chapter 2. That's where the action begins.

How could I skip to chapter 2? Yes, my spiritual coma was beginning to lift, but I still felt like I had fallen and pieces of me were strewn everywhere. How could I put it all together again?

thirty-five

Although they are broken vessels, bruised in this world . . . the Holy One makes use only of them.

ZOHAR II 218A

ONE DAY in February 2004 as I was sitting in a waiting room, I was leafing through a magazine when I saw an ad for a china company, and I was flooded by a rush of memory.

We didn't have a whole lot of money when I was growing up, but I never knew it. I was the youngest of four children and to me life was perfect. Our home was always filled with laughter and music and lots of good food. At our holiday table there were always aunts and uncles and cousins and grandparents and lots of great stories. But I do remember that our holiday dishes were a sorry sight, a collection of hand-me-downs. There were some plates with pink stripes, some with silver trim, others with gold trim.

One year just before Rosh Hashanah, the Jewish New Year, when I was eight, my parents saved up the money to buy their very first set of china. It was a closeout set, on final sale. Oh, my mother loved those dishes. I remember her excitement as she carefully unwrapped each piece and put it away in the cabinet. On the eve of Rosh Hashanah

143

my mother proudly set the table with her new china. The room looked positively royal. All the dishes sparkled and there were even matching serving pieces. My mother lit the candles with gratitude for all the blessings of the New Year, my father said the blessings over the wine and bread, and we sat down to an incredible meal.

After dinner my parents went next door to my grandparents' house and all four of us children stayed home and cleaned up in the kitchen. My sister, Mimi, who was nineteen, was washing the dishes; my brother Danny, who was sixteen, was drying them; my brother David, who was fourteen, and who, by the way, was always picking on me, was putting the china back in the cabinet. And I was helping him.

And then it happened.

A single plate slipped out of my hand and it landed on a whole pile of other dishes and shattered them to pieces. The whole thing took a split second, but in that second I broke twelve pieces of my mother's precious brand-new china. Two dinner plates, three salad plates, two teacups, one saucer, three soup bowls, and the lid to the sugar bowl.

We all just stood there and stared at the shattered china. I couldn't remember my house ever being that quiet. Then my brother David, who was always picking on me, said, "Boy, are you in trouble. When Mom gets home she's going to kill you." "But it was an accident," I said in my defense, "it was an accident."

Instantly my sister, Mimi, the oldest of us, moved into action. She said, "We've got to get rid of these broken dishes. When Mom comes home we can't let her see this." So Mimi found a cardboard box and she swept everything up by herself, cleaned up the whole mess, and put it outside with the trash.

I thought Mimi was right. The smashed dishes would have been a horrible sight for my parents to come home to. But just the same, with each passing minute I got sicker and sicker with dread. My head was spinning, my stomach was in knots, my heart was racing. Then my brother David, who was always picking on me, went outside to the trash and brought back the box of broken dishes. I looked at him. What was he doing? Was he trying to get me into bigger trouble? Was he going to show my mother all the broken pieces and say, "Look, Mom, see what Nomi did"?

David took the box of broken china, brought it to his room, and spread the shards all over his desk. Then he took out a tube of Duco Cement and began work on the most difficult jigsaw puzzle I had ever seen. He worked slowly and methodically. A half hour passed and he had the two dinner plates back together. Another half hour and the teacups were done. I kept running back to the front door to see if my parents were coming, then I'd run back to him and watch him at work. As I watched him, I thought to myself, *I can't believe David wants to help me.* For a moment I let myself believe David could glue the dishes back together so well that my mom would never be able to tell they'd been broken. Well, that's not exactly how it played out.

My parents came home around 11:00 p.m., and I had to gather up all my courage and tell my mother what I had done. I can still see the combination of hurt and anger that spread across my mother's face at that moment. Then I brought her to David's room. His desk was still covered with shattered china, but on the right side of his desk there was a row of pieces he had already repaired. When my mother saw all the trouble David had gone to just to protect me from getting into trouble, she was moved. David stayed up till 2:30 a.m. putting all the pieces back together again. And because of him my mother never yelled at me and never punished me. All she said was, "Nomi, you have to learn to be more careful next time."

David saved me that night, but he saved me not by miraculously erasing the damage I had caused. He saved me by caring. By making the effort to repair what I had broken.

My parents never replaced the china I had shattered. They couldn't afford a new set, and the set they had was the last of its kind. So year after year at every holiday, my mother set the table with her favorite china, including all the pieces I'd broken that David had glued together. They didn't look perfect—you could see the jagged scars across the shiny white surface of each piece he had repaired—but you could still eat off of them. And the sugar inside the sugar bowl was still sweet.

Often it's when things break that we learn the greatest lessons about ourselves, about those around us, and about God, too.

My whole life I was plagued with guilt over those broken dishes. It was only when I started to study Kabala, Jewish mysticism, that I learned that as a dish breaker I was actually in very good company.

You don't have to look very hard to notice that God didn't give us a perfect world. There are cracks everywhere. Awful diseases, natural disasters; there's war and poverty and evil in this world. The great Jewish mystic Rabbi Isaac Luria, who was known as the ARI, offered this explanation as to why the world is so broken. He taught that when God was creating the world, God sent forth a stream of holy emanations that flowed into vessels that were created to contain God's holy light. But something went wrong. The emanations that flowed from God were too powerful for the vessels. And the vessels shattered. In Hebrew he called this moment Shevirat Hakelim, which means, literally, "the shattering of the dishes."

So God broke the dishes and the shards from the shattered vessels got scattered throughout the cosmos. The ARI said we live in a broken world littered with those fragments. The broken shards are everywhere around us, even within our own souls. And those shards aren't just garbage to be thrown out, they contain holy sparks, entrapped divine light. Our task on earth is to repair the world by finding those fragments and restoring them to wholeness.

The ARI's lesson was clear: We can't repair the spiritual brokenness of this world like my brother David did with a tube of Duco Cement. We can only repair creation by caring, by seeking to live up to our highest potential, by uncovering the secret holiness that's hidden in our ordinary lives.

I thought to myself, *Perhaps God is waiting for us to notice what is broken in this world and in our own souls. But it's hard to put things back together again. So sometimes, instead of exercising our own power to fix things, we give over our power to people who take advantage of us or let us down.*

Five years earlier a man named Steve had called me. I knew him well; I had married him and his wife, Annie. Steve was crazy about Annie. His voice on the phone sounded shaky. I asked, "What's wrong, Steve?" He said he was worried about his marriage. When I asked what the matter with his marriage was, he said, "The whole thing's crazy, and I'm embarrassed to even tell you what the problem is." Eventually Steve shared his problem with me.

Annie was feeling a little lost, so her friend told her to see a psychic. Just for fun really, Annie went to a psychic named Magda. Magda read Annie's palm and told her, "I see a break in your marriage line. You're going to get divorced." After that Annie was a mess. She made Steve come with her the next day to see Magda, and Magda looked at his palm and pronounced, "There is a break in your marriage line too. There's a divorce in your future."

Steve said to me, "I feel so stupid, Rabbi. I'm a rational person.

I'm a doctor. But Magda's got me and Annie all freaked out. We were planning to try to have a baby this year, but now Annie doesn't think we *should*, because we *might* be getting a divorce."

The next morning Steve and Annie showed up in my study. They looked nervous and scared. I asked them to close their eyes and hold out their palms. Then I took out my pen and started writing on their hands. They started to giggle because it tickled, but I kept writing. Then I asked them to open their eyes and read their palms. This is what I had written: "Your future isn't written on your hands, your future is in your hands."

Remembering Steve and Annie, I thought to myself, *There are always going to be people who just can't wait to give us negative news. People who just can't wait to close doors for us. This world is full of Magdas who predict our doom, who tell us what we'll never be, what we can never become.*

There were doctors who told us Noa would slowly degenerate and die. There were teachers who told us Noa would never be able to learn. I spent sleepless nights worrying every time Noa came down with the slightest cold. I was sure this was the beginning of the end. Yes, this world was full of Magdas.

A friend of mine was hired to be an assistant rabbi in a very traditional congregation. She discovered pretty quickly that this wasn't exactly a perfect fit. She wanted to lead informal discussions; the senior rabbi wanted her to deliver formal sermons.

One day she went to the senior rabbi and had a heart-to-heart talk with him. She asked him, "Tell me, where do you think I belong?" He said to her, "First of all, your voice is too nasal and it gets on people's nerves." Before I share the rest of the rabbi's remarks, I have to mention that God happens to have blessed my friend with very large breasts. Okay, they're huge breasts. Now back to the rabbi.

"And second of all," he continued, "your breasts are too large. I think it's distracting to people to have to see such large breasts on the pulpit." Finally, he concluded, "I think you belong in a small town somewhere where you can preach to ten or twenty people. That's all you can hope for."

My friend was devastated by this heartless assessment of her. Had she truly internalized this rabbi's words, she might have just curled up in a ball and given up her life as a rabbi. But somehow she knew he was wrong. She became the rabbi of a large congregation of Jews who respect and treasure her nasal teaching, and who eagerly look forward to seeing her big breasts on the pulpit each week.

I told myself, *Yes, there are people in this world who don't believe in us, who don't appreciate us.* But sometimes Magda's voice is inside our own heads: *Nothing's going my way. I'll never get this job. I'll never fall in love again. I'll never heal. I'll never get out of this rut. Nothing will ever change.*

I asked myself, *Whose voice is that inside our heads?* And then I found my answer: *It doesn't matter whose voice it is. Don't listen to it! I can promise you one thing. It's not God's voice. Do you think God is saying to us, "You're a schlemiel, you're a loser, you'll never amount to anything"? God is saying, "I believe in you. I made you. I know what you're capable of."*

The true repair for the brokenness in our souls is the belief that we have the power to change and grow. The Magdas of this world may tell us our fates are sealed, but nothing is sealed.

I took out a piece of paper and began writing on the coffee table in the waiting room: *If you listen to Magda's voice you'll get stuck, you'll be paralyzed with fear. If you listen to God's voice, your whole life will open up before you.*

Soon I was writing words of encouragement: *Nomi, if there's something broken in your life, don't just throw the shards out with the trash, bring the box back inside and face the jagged pieces. Examine them carefully and answers will start to surface. Will there be a seamless, perfect healing? Probably not. There will always be cracks. But our challenge in life is to learn how to live with our scars, because our scars are holy. They are a seat of wisdom within us. It's from them that we learn our strength, our compassion. It's from them that we learn how to pray, how to dream, how to listen, how to reach out and offer help.*

And then, as I was sitting in the waiting room writing furiously all over my piece of paper, I added these words: *If you're having trouble figuring out how to accomplish this, how to put the broken pieces back together, remember you don't have to do it alone. Lean on someone you can trust, ask for help and help will come.*

It had been a long time since I smashed my mother's dishes. My children were older than I was when I broke the dishes. Over the years, whenever I saw a sign for an estate sale or whenever I passed by an antique shop, I'd instinctively pull my car over just to see if by some chance my mother's dishes might be there for sale. Whenever I passed through the china section of a department store, I'd always keep my eyes open for my mother's dishes even though her pattern was a closeout a long, long time before.

And then that day in February as I was sitting in the waiting room reading an article in a magazine, I came upon a small ad for a company that replaced old china pieces. I knew it was a long shot, but I just had to call. I dialed the number and a receptionist with a strong southern accent picked up. "Lorraine speaking. How can I help you?" I asked sheepishly, "I was wondering, have you ever heard of a china pattern called Andante by a company called Sango?" "No, I have not," Lorraine replied cheerfully, "but thank you for calling and you have a nice day."

I was just about to say thank you and hang up, but instead I said,

"Lorraine, do you have a minute? Can I tell you a story?" "Sure, honey, you go right ahead," she responded. Suddenly I began spilling my soul to this telephone receptionist. "Lorraine," I said, "when I was a little girl I broke my mother's china." I told her all about my brother David and the Duco Cement. I told her how my mother was a widow, and getting on in years, and how she still served all her holiday meals on those same dishes. Lorraine started sniffling and blowing her nose right in my ear. She said, "You stick with me, darlin'. I am going to find you those dishes for your sweet mother. I am going to turn this world upside down to find you those pieces."

Two months later there was a package at my door. Lorraine had found a single dinner plate. A few weeks later another plate arrived. Then more and more packages started coming. Six months later I opened a package from Lorraine. It was the final missing piece: the lid to the sugar bowl.

I called Lorraine up to thank her. I said, "Sometimes God works miracles all alone, but today God worked through a shining woman named Lorraine." She blew her nose right in my ear and sniffled, "Go on and give those dishes to your mother already before you break 'em again, you hear?"

My mother came to visit me that August. On her birthday I placed a big cardboard box in front of her. "Nomi, you didn't have to get me anything," she said. I said to her, "Mom, it's a couple of years overdue, but it's never too late to set things straight." My mother looked puzzled. Then she leaned over and opened up the box. How can I possibly describe the emotions that passed between us? I can still see the combination of laughter and tears that spread across her face at that moment.

That night, when the house was dark, I sat at my kitchen table smiling as I wrote these words: *We live in a broken world. Inside us there beats a heart that has been broken more times than we'd care to remember, but there will always be someone to help us pick up the shattered pieces and begin the process of repair. Sometimes with glue, sometimes with love, sometimes with miracles. Always with God.*

tHirty-six

Seek advice but use your own common sense.

YIDDISH PROVERB

LORRAINE WAS a gift from God, but now there were two new
Magdas in my life.

I tried hard to block out my memories of the cognitive assessments Noa went through at that time. Even now it's difficult for me
to think back on those days with Dr. Lapp and Dr. Lowe.

Dr. Lapp was a developmental specialist. We turned to her to
assess the workings of Noa's mind. Noa spent several hours on several days being a good sport. And then Rob and I came to meet her.
I was expecting her to say that Noa just needed more time to develop
and grow. Dr. Lapp looked at us with a sour expression; I instinctively started defending Noa. She was telling me Noa had significant
cognitive deficits. I was telling her how wise Noa was. She told me
with clear frustration in her voice, "I showed her a picture of a wagon
and she called it a dragon." I thought, *At least it rhymes. Maybe Noa will
be a poet.* I remembered once showing Noa a breathtaking photo of a
young Pakistani woman bedecked in white robes against a clear blue

sky. She said to me, "The woman is dressed in clouds." Yes, perhaps a poet.

Then Dr. Lapp added, "And I listened to her heart and I heard a definite blowing sound. There is a certain disease that affects the brain and the heart. You need to see a cardiologist right away."

Rob and I drove home utterly demoralized and panicked. In the morning I raced Noa to a pediatric cardiologist. He examined her, ran some tests, and said, "That doctor needs to check her hearing. There's nothing wrong with this child's heart."

I began to question Dr. Lapp's assessment of Noa. If she misdiagnosed her heart, perhaps she misdiagnosed her mind too. I wanted a second opinion.

So now I dragged Noa to Dr. Lowe. She was a neuropsychologist who saw patients in her home. Noa and I snooped around the living room while the doctor was running late. The place was an absolute mess. Every surface was covered with piles of paper and files. The entire dining room table was inundated with papers and folders, the kitchen was overflowing with unwashed plates, the steps to the second floor were lined with stacks of newspapers and magazines. A sour smell of old orange juice and old milk filled the air. I am certainly not a neat person by any stretch of the imagination, but this place was bordering on disgusting.

And then I saw the photos of this doctor's daughter who had just graduated as valedictorian from a prestigeous law school.

Dr. Lowe assessed Noa for several hours on several days and Noa was such a good sport. Then I came in one afternoon to discuss her findings. She told me she'd never encountered a child quite like Noa before who could score so poorly on one scale and relatively well on another. She didn't exactly have high hopes for Noa's future. With a pout on her face she said, "I know how you're feeling." I thought to myself, *Your daughter was the valedictorian of her law school and you know how I'm feeling? What do you know about me and my feelings?* And then she offered me a crumb of comfort. She told me most kids like Noa function very poorly, but Noa had . . . she was searching for a word to describe what Noa had. She rubbed the fingers of her right hand together, as if she were pinching salt, and said, "Noa has a spark."

Okay, then. I'd have to hang my hopes on a pinch of salt and a spark.

In the meantime I decided I would not pull Noa out of her school where she was happy and had friends.

tHIRty-seveN

A dream is one-sixtieth of prophecy.
THE TALMUD BERACHOT 57B

I WAS reeling from my meetings with Dr. Lapp and Dr. Lowe. It was a Friday morning and I was on my way to meet Toba for our weekly Torah study. I tried to put on a happy face, but when we sat down to study I broke down and wept. "I just don't believe it. I don't believe Noa is that severely impaired." Toba was comforting me, telling me about her friend Erica's son, who has been through cognitive testing as well. She told me Erica had found a great doctor in New York. She encouraged me to go on a pilgrimage to see him. She gave me Erica's phone number.

We cracked open our books and came upon this teaching from the Talmud: "Who is the wise person? One who can see the new moon in the dark night." I imagined this quote was telling me it's possible to see in the darkness a glimmer of hope. To see how the world is now, and to sense how it can be. The moon may be hidden from sight, but we have the power to envision the great light that's in store for us.

Maybe that's what "Noa has a spark" meant. Maybe I needed to envision how that spark would one day burn brightly.

I asked Toba to wait a moment and wrote these thoughts in my journal: *The power of vision is the power to believe we will find our way when the road before us is foggy and uncertain. It's the power to believe even in the midst of sadness, pain, exhaustion, and fear that you will have cause to celebrate again.*

I don't need to accept what the doctors say. I don't need to make peace with things the way they are, I need to start dreaming about the way things can be.

And then Toba and I came upon a second teaching, a rabbinic commentary about Miriam the Prophet, who was the sister of Moses. The Bible says when the Children of Israel crossed to the other side of the Red Sea, Miriam and all the women took out their drums and started singing to God and dancing. The commentary asked: If the Israelites fled Egypt in such a rush that they didn't even have time to let their bread rise, where did the women get all those drums from? The answer given was: When the Jews were rushing to leave Egypt, Miriam told all the women to pack their drums. She said, "Things may look frightening right now, but trust me, you will have cause to celebrate!"

Suddenly I remembered what my kids were doing the night Dr. Becket called me with that horrible diagnosis. While I was sitting on my bedroom floor sobbing, they were running around the living room with drums and spoons. There would be cause to celebrate.

Here's how my journal entry continued: *The rabbis teach us that everyone has a bit of a prophet inside them. They say that a dream is one-sixtieth of prophecy. Everyone has the power to perceive the new moon in the darkened sky. That's what the Prophet Joel understood when he said, "Your sons and daughters shall prophesy; your old shall dream dreams, and your young shall see visions."*

I wanted to start dreaming. I was looking for the moon. I was packing my drum.

thirty-eight

And the angel of God spoke to me.

GENESIS 31:11

T HE VERY next week as I was sitting in the waiting room at the
clinic where Noa received physical, occupational, and speech
therapy, a bald, jovial man with rosy cheeks struck up a conversation
with me. I had noticed him before on my visits, but we had never spoken. He told me about his son, who could not speak words and could
only make squeaking sounds. I described Noa's various physical and
cognitive challenges. I told him how worried I was about her.

He looked at me with the delighted smile of the Buddha and said,
"I've been watching your daughter for some weeks now, and I want
you to know that she is something special. She's got the real thing,
that rare quality. She's going to surpass you; she'll put you both to
shame—you and your husband. She's going to leave you in the dust.
She's going to be so far ahead of you that she will achieve things you
won't even be able to dream of. When that day arrives, just remember
that I was the one who told you so."

My eyes started to tear up. I had been sitting in the waiting room worrying about Noa, and this extraordinary man transformed my thinking. This man told me my daughter would shine. He delivered a prophecy of hope. Instead of worrying about the future, I needed to start looking forward to it eagerly.

Yes, there were Magdas in my life who predicted Noa's doom, but this angel appeared in my life and taught me to hope.

tHiRty-niNe

If you lie on the ground, you can't fall.
YIDDISH PROVERB

I PHONED Toba's friend Erica that night. Erica told me about an amazing specialist, Dr. Bloom in New York. She said he had taught her to see her son's strength and was helping her son see his own strength. "Tell me about Noa's strengths," she asked. I told Erica about Noa's kindness, how perceptive and wise she was. I told her Noa was a good friend, extremely social. I talked about Noa's sense of humor and her serenity and optimism. "That's what you have to focus on," she said. "Focus on her strengths, teach her to see her strengths." She said Dr. Bloom had changed her son's life. She gave me the brain guru's number, warned me about the long waiting list to get in, and told me I should call every week to see if I could get an appointment.

I was feeling . . . hopeful. Was a small place in my heart starting to believe the bald angel? That Noa was going to be okay? I didn't even know what "okay" meant. But I was starting to believe that she was going to live. I so wanted to believe it. And I wanted to believe that she was going to be happy. That her strength would increase. That her learning would improve.

As that faith grew, I began dreaming about returning to my rabbinic calling. I knew I had so much to give, so much to teach, so much to say. But I just didn't quite have the courage to take the plunge.

Sometimes you think you want something, but you don't want it badly enough to actually risk discomfort for it. As the Yiddish proverb goes, "The cat likes fish, but she doesn't want to wet her paws." And sometimes you want something badly, but still there are forces preventing you from taking action. Forces that keep you standing on the dock when you so want to jump in the water and start swimming.

Sometimes, every once in a while, you get lucky and somebody gives you a push just at that moment when you need it the most. You're standing there hesitating on the dock and someone just pushes you into the water—not in a cruel way, but in a way of caring.

Thinking of my brother Danny always calls to mind the word "push." He's eight years older than I am, and the two stories I remember most when I look back on my own childhood with him are both times when he pushed me.

The first story: I was eight, he was sixteen. My sister, Mimi, was visiting Israel at the time, and she mailed me a beautiful silver ring with my Hebrew name engraved on it. I was so excited to receive this present from her, but when I tried on the ring I saw that it was too small for me.

Danny said, "Let me see that ring." He looked at it. "It's not too small for you." He took my hand and pushed the ring on my finger. "You see, it fits," he said.

But it didn't take very long for me to realize that I couldn't get the ring off. "Danny, the ring's stuck. I can't get it off."

"Nonsense," he said.

He pulled and he tugged. Nothing. Then he took soap. Nothing. Then oil. Nothing. Ice cubes. Nothing. Soon my finger started to turn purple and it started swelling up. And Danny turned white.

My mom came home. It was seven o'clock on a Friday night, and I remember walking with her from store to store until we found the only jeweler still open, who had to cut that ring right off my finger. My mom still has that cut ring. She's saved it all these years.

Danny's first push . . . not that helpful.

Nine years passed. Now I was seventeen and Danny was twenty-five and in his fourth year of medical school. A year and a half earlier our father had been murdered. My three older siblings were all adults who had moved out of the house years before.

A house once full of noise and laughter and celebration and music with four kids running around and two parents madly in love had fallen silent. And now it was just me and my mom living alone in our pain and mourning.

It was my senior year of high school and I was supposed to be thinking about moving out and going off to college. But I couldn't think at all and my mother was in no state of mind to help me. There was no college tour for me. No one telling me where to apply.

And, of course, there were so many mixed emotions. My mom wanted me to go off to school, but she also wanted me at home. I was her baby, her comfort. I wanted to leave her, but I couldn't bear the guilt of leaving my mother to live by herself all alone.

As a mother myself now, I understand what my mother was going through. Last year Adi decided to go for a semester abroad in Israel. He was only in tenth grade at the time, only fifteen years old. And part of me wanted him to go and have a great learning experience. But a much bigger part of me wanted him to stay home.

In the end, Adi went and I missed him so much that I took to wearing his sweatshirts and T-shirts every single day. Noa, who is a total fashion queen, told me, "Mom, you've got to stop wearing Adiwear." One day she said, "If someone gave me a choice between what you're wearing right now and death, I'd pick death." She even wrote away to the TV show *What Not to Wear* and said, "Help! You've got to help my mom. She only wears my brother's T-shirts. Teach her how to dress."

Back in the fall of my senior year in high school, I could so see the possibility of never leaving my mother. I could so understand the fate of the unlucky child who somehow gets sucked into the vortex of a family problem and can't seem to ever be free of it.

Right across the street from my childhood home there was a family like that. The Kisilevskys. Mama Kisilevsky was in her nineties and she lived with her three grown children, who were in their sixties. The three children—Anna, Harry, and Florence—had never left home. Maybe I would never leave home . . .

It was December 29, the day before my brother Danny's wedding. He drove down from Boston with Sue, his bride-to-be. There was so much to take care of just a day before the wedding. So many plans to finalize—table seating, dealing with the rabbi, the florist, the caterer, and on and on.

Danny came into the living room and said to me, "Hey, kiddo, how are those college applications going?" I sat there frozen on the couch. He repeated, "How's it going with the applications?" I looked at him with a blank stare. "I didn't do it. I don't know where to apply, I don't know what to say, I didn't apply anywhere."

"Nomi, when are they due?"

"January 1."

The next thing I knew, Danny was rummaging around in the basement. And then he came back up with my mom's baby blue Brother manual typewriter. He set up a card table in the middle of our living room and my soon-to-be sister-in-law Sue was sitting at the table with the typewriter and Danny was pacing back and forth and dictating as she typed.

Together they filled out all the forms. And then Danny wrote my college essay. It was all about recombinant DNA. I tell you, I didn't understand a word of it. I just sat on the couch like a lost sheep.

This went on all day long, the day before Danny's wedding. Danny dictating, Sue typing, me watching. By nightfall all the applications were sealed and stamped and ready to go.

And Danny never said to me, "What's wrong with you?" Or "Why did you wait so long?" He never said anything really.

But in his eyes I understood what he was trying to say to me. He was saying, *Nomi, go. It's time for you to go. It's time to start living. I'm giving you permission to go. Go out that door. Go to college, learn, live your life, have fun. Go!*

Danny's first push . . . not that helpful.

His second push saved my life.

Remembering Danny and his push, I thought about how hard it is to leave a world you're familiar with. It's hard to press on into an unknown future. But living on the dock isn't really living, is it?

Danny got me into Cornell University. For some time I was ashamed to tell anyone he had filled out my application and written my essay for me. But I'm okay with it now. I'm okay with the way the whole story is unfolding still.

Danny likes to say that he didn't get into Cornell the first time he applied, when he was in high school, but he got in the second time.

And I've tried to repay the favor. When it was time for all three of his children's Bar and Bat Mitzvahs, I helped each one of them with their speeches and I delivered the sermon at each of their services. And when each of his kids applied to college, I helped each one of them with their essays.

Now I began thinking of Noa's needs. I asked myself, *What sort of push does she need?* I knew I wasn't doing her any favors by keeping her in a school that had no expertise in special education. But how could I rip her away from her friends and her prayers? How could I let go of my fantasy that Noa would magically catch up with her classmates? Perhaps that was the push she needed. Perhaps she would flourish in a school with teachers who could understand how to teach her. Perhaps.

Sometimes you get lucky and somebody gives you a push at the moment when you need it the most.

Every new life begins with something as simple as a push.

And I was about to get the push I needed.

It's Time

forty

When fortune calls, offer her a chair.

YIDDISH PROVERB

Do you miss it?" I heard my friend Norma asking me. It was late April, just a couple of weeks after I met the bald man who spoke the prophecy of hope. I was sitting at a bakery having breakfast with my friends Carol and Norma. I didn't know what Norma was talking about. She asked me again, "Do you miss it?" "Miss what?" I asked. She meant did I miss leading a community in prayer. I froze. I wasn't planning to go so deep that morning. I just wanted coffee and a Danish. Now I had to look at the way I dropped the ball in the middle of my rabbinate, how I retired in the middle of my career.

I said, "I don't miss everything, but I miss some things." Carol jumped in, "What do you miss, Nomi?" I breathed and thought for a moment, "I guess what I miss most is leading people in prayer on Friday as the sun is setting and the Sabbath comes. It's magic. I miss spreading that magic."

"If you could lead a service today, what would it look like?" Norma asked me. I thought for a moment about what I would do. I thought about all the Jews I knew who were turned off by Judaism. Jews who walked away from prayer life because they found Judaism spiritually unfulfilling. Jews who walked away from prayer because they were raised on God-As-Superman and not on The God Who Sees Me. I said, "It would be a place for those who are searching for spiritual nourishment, who want to be transformed. I would write a whole new English translation of the Hebrew service. There would be a band, lots of uplifting music."

For a moment I found myself daydreaming, humming a Sabbath prayer to myself.

"It's time," I heard Carol say. "Time for what?" I asked her. "It's time for you to lead a Sabbath service again."

I wanted to dismiss Carol, to change the subject. But she and Norma wouldn't let up. They were excited. "Where do you want the service to be?" Norma asked. "How often do you want to do it?" Carol added. I fantasized, "The first Friday of every month." *What am I talking about? I can't lead a service. I barely pulled it together to be at this breakfast today. I'm too worried about Noa. I've got to fight a new battle with the school district. I can't. I'm overwhelmed, lost, confused, drowning.*

"What are you talking about?" I finally said out loud. "I don't have a sanctuary, I don't have a congregation, I don't have any money, I don't have any prayer books." They looked unconcerned. Carol said, "Say you'll do it and we'll take care of the rest."

I didn't say "Yes." I'm pretty sure I said, "We'll see," which is my way of saying no without having to say no.

Driving home, I was reeling from the conversation I'd just had. I was talking to myself: *I would need to put together a whole committee just to find a sanctuary to hold the service in. It's too overwhelming . . .* but it was fun to dream about it anyway.

At home I was about to forget about the whole thing and put it behind me when some force inside me said, "Just do one thing." So I sat down at Adi's computer and I Googled: "Houses of Worship Los Angeles." Up came a list of some three thousand congregations. Already I was defeated. I was ready to give up and put this crazy idea out of my mind. I sat down on Adi's bed and closed my eyes. That voice inside me persisted, "Just do one thing. Call one place."

An image appeared before my eyes. A church popped into my head. It was a church I always passed when I was on my way to visit patients in the hospital. It always calmed me. Over the years whenever I went to visit the sick, I'd pass that church, take a deep breath, and find an inner center of strength to pray with people clinging to life in the ICU.

I decided to call that one church. I dialed the number and someone picked up. I said nervously, "Is the reverend in?" The voice on the other end said, "This is she." *Wow,* I thought to myself, *this is interesting.* I said, "I'm Naomi Levy, I'm a rabbi." I was stumbling all over my words, I'm not sure I was making any sense. I heard myself say, "I was wondering if you might be open to the idea of having a bunch of Jews pray in your church once a month." *Did I just say, "Bunch of Jews"?* There was dead silence on the other end. "Are you calling me because you know my husband is Jewish?" I heard her ask. "No, I definitely wouldn't have guessed that," I replied. She said, "Well, my husband *is* Jewish, and nothing would make me happier than to have a Shabbat service in my church."

I couldn't believe this was happening. I said, "Well, if you're open to the idea, let me go get my calendar so we can set a time to get together." I put down the phone for a second and my heart was pounding as I grabbed my calendar and got back on the line.

"When would you like me to come to meet you?" I asked.

"Now," she said.

"Now? What do you mean now?"

She said, "Come now."

I said, "But I'm in my sweatpants and I look like a slob."

"Come now," she said. "Like a slob."

I hung up the phone, picked up my car keys, and walked out the front door in a daze.

I drove to the church in a trance. I found the reverend's office, opened the door. We looked at each other—complete strangers—and we both gasped. "Oh my God!" is all that came out. That's what she said too, "Oh my God!" We just kept repeating those three words. She got up from behind her desk and we walked toward each other; we fell into each other's arms. We just stood there holding each other in silence. Oh my God. How can I describe what happened? There was this instant, intense connection. An indescribable sense of recognition. A soul recognition. I'd never had a meeting like this with anyone, ever. Looking at her was like looking at myself.

She took me by the hand and led me to the church's sanctuary. It was beautiful, all wooden, Mission style. It was exactly the kind of space I was dreaming of for the service. We sat on a wooden bench holding hands. "I've known you my entire life," she said. "I know," I replied. There were tears in our eyes. We were cut from the same cloth, kindred souls of different faiths. We didn't have to say very much. It was all so obvious and beyond words.

Her name is Reverend Kirsten Linford.

* * *

Suddenly I flashed on that day in the boutique when the saleswoman kept calling me Mara. Was it possible that back then Kirsten was already imprinted on my soul? Could this moment be part of the good that was already waiting for me?

Kirsten opened the doors of her church to me and my dreams. So many other doors were opening all at once. I couldn't have prayed for this, for her. How could I have known such a blessing was even possible?

An engine turned on inside me. I started dreaming of a new model for a Jewish community. I started listening to Jews who had walked away from synagogues. I pictured an experimental community that had no dues, no membership, no tickets, no movement affiliation. Soon Rob and I and nine friends were dreaming together. Rob's parents were dreaming with us as well. We all met around our dining room table. Rob helped me set the agenda, and he told me to believe I could once again share my passion for Judaism with others. Brett offered his legal counsel and volunteered to manage our finances. Carol would take on social justice work. Andie would handle publicity. Rob's dad and Andie's husband, Warren, would help with business ideas. Rob would help with publicity and he would also cater the meal after the service. He quoted Napoleon, "An army marches on its stomach." In order to hold a Jewish service in Kirsten's church, there was a huge cross we would need to cover. Wanda, a gifted artist, created a beautiful banner for the pulpit. Her husband, Avi, would help raise funds. Dan would be our president. Helene and Carin and Sari, my mother-in-law, would help get us organized. Helene's husband, Rich, set up our Web site.

We talked about a new approach to Jewish life. "A Soulful Community of Prayer in Action" became our motto. We wanted to revive deep spirituality, and we wanted to link it with social justice, with actions that can heal our world. Every prayer service would be linked to a day of action. We all chipped in and created a small pool of funds. It was April; we decided to hold our first service in June.

Ideas for melodies started popping into my head as I drove carpool. My friend Andie, a trained vocalist, started singing with me. She would sing at the service. I began looking for musicians. My friend Mike Stein is a cantor and a brilliant musician. I called and asked him if he knew any musicians to recommend to me. He started giving me names, I wrote them down. The next day Mike called me back. He said, "Naomi, my two sons are musicians. I didn't give you their names because I didn't want you to feel obligated to hire them." I said, "Mike, don't worry, I'd just like to meet them." Mike gave me the phone numbers of his sons, Justin and Jared. When I met these brothers I was simply speechless. They were exactly the people I had been hoping for. So talented, so soulful. We started to put together a band. Jamie, a Middle Eastern drummer, became our percussionist. Fino would play lead guitar. Alula, an Ethiopan Jewish refugee, would be on percussion as well. Kirsten gave me the names of two incredible people from the church's choir. Ed became our pianist and Bernadette would play violin and sing. The band was interracial, interfaith, and unbelievably talented. We created a Jewish service with music from all over the world. I felt like Dorothy in *The Wizard of Oz*; I felt like I was in a dream surrounded by all these amazing people who all seemed oddly familiar, as if I had known them all along.

A name for this community came to me: Nashuva. It means "We Will Return." I thought about how we all have the need to return—to passion, to our dreams, to our essential goodness, to love, to our own souls, to our God. We spend so much time striving to succeed, or simply manage the chaos in our lives, that we rarely make the time to reflect and uncover our true possibility. Our souls hunger for more. The name Nashuva implied a haven from the hectic lives we lead. A place where people could leave behind their worries, receive the spiritual infusion they were looking for, and emerge transformed. Nashuva would be a time to pray, to sing, to be still and listen to the voice of your soul. But the goal of prayer wasn't only personal peace. At Nashuva prayer would lead to action. Nashuva would become a service that led to service.

Of course, We Will Return meant something very special to me. I was returning to my calling, to my passion, and to my God-given gift. And I could see that Noa was returning to the toughness that had been hiding inside her. I kept telling myself there wasn't a deadly disease waiting for the right moment to overtake her, there was only a light waiting for the right moment to shine. I repeated the bald man's prophecy often in my heart: "She's going to surpass you."

I started writing a whole new prayer book inspired by the traditional Jewish Friday night service. I wrote a prayer about transformation:

> *Sometimes liberation takes a lifetime,*
> *Sometimes liberation can happen in an instant.*
> *Seas part,*
> *Gates open,*
> *Our awareness expands,*
> *And we are filled with awe ...*

"You unlock doors I never thought would open" was the last line of the prayer. I hadn't written anything in quite some time. The words were flowing out of me now. Prayers, psalms. I wrote prayers as I sat in the waiting rooms of Noa's therapies. I wrote prayers as I sat in the dark watching behind a two-way mirror as Noa received therapies that were making her grow stronger and stronger.

It was the first Friday in June. The night of our first service. I was petrified. Adi sensed this. He told me not to worry. "Mom, it's going to be amazing. You'll see," he assured me.

In the car on the way to the service, Noa started singing the prayers to me. Her high-pitched voice filled me with hope.

My friend Dina was helping to set up. She wanted to know how many people to expect. I told her to set out twenty prayer books.

It was moments before the service. I was upstairs in the Bride's Room praying. I saw Kirsten and I realized I needed something from her. "Can you bless me?" I asked. We both stood up. Kirsten put her hands on my head and closed her eyes. I closed my eyes too as she prayed: "God, be with my soul sister Nomi as she is about to lead this community in prayer. Be with her. Let Your light shine through her and let it light up those in need of light. Let this community unite, lifting each other up in beautiful song and in prayers of hope and healing. Bless this rabbi, God, my soul sister Nomi."

I could feel the voice of Kirsten's prayer entering my heart. It calmed me.

The service began. People kept coming. Everyone in the room seemed to be rising up. As if we were all breathing in helium. I saw people praying and crying. Beaming and weeping. So many tears, so much light. Hundreds of people were packed in the church now. People were standing in the aisles.

I talked about the word *Nashuva,* what it means to return to something new, a homecoming that is life-altering.

You unlock doors I never thought would open. Yes.

forty-one

A heavenly voice issues from Mount Horeb every day . . .
Exodus Rabbah XLI: 7

A LL SORTS of doors were opening. My book *Talking to God* was published. I was getting phone calls and I was actually answering them. I was saying yes to speaking requests. Now I was leading a spiritual community and also giving lectures again around the country.

In late September I was lecturing as a scholar-in-residence at a synagogue in North Carolina. The administrator at the synagogue had prearranged a car to take me to the airport at 6:00 a.m. on Sunday. When I got back to my hotel Saturday night I looked at my ticket and realized I didn't have to be at the airport quite that early, so I called the car service and asked to change my pickup time to 6:30 a.m.

In the morning when I got into the car at six thirty, the driver said, "I've been waiting here since six." I said, "Didn't you get the call that I changed the time?" He told me he hadn't. I apologized and assured him I had in fact made the call the night before. The driver nodded and asked, "When did you get the call?" I was thinking, "Six? Six thirty?" And then I realized he meant: "When did I get the CALL?"

I thought to myself, *Christians speak about the call with such ease.* The truth is, Jews don't usually talk about getting a call. Rabbis become rabbis because they want to. I remembered when I was sitting on the admissions committee for the Jewish Theological Seminary. All day long we interviewed young people who wanted to become rabbis. We read their essays. We asked them all the same question: Why do you want to be a rabbi? And you could almost predict the answers: *Because I love teaching Torah. Because I love Jews and Judaism and I want to lead people into a life of prayer and Torah . . .*

But one rabbinical candidate walked in and when we asked, "Why do you want to be a rabbi?" this student replied, "Because I've had very strong visions that my soul was at the foot of Mount Sinai at the time of the giving of the Torah." When that interview was over, all of us on the admissions committee looked at one another and rolled our eyes as if to say, "That was weird."

And then the dean of the rabbinical school asked, "Why shouldn't we take the idea of calling seriously?" Of course he was right. And we did admit the student whose soul was there at Sinai.

I believed we all get the call, but I also understood how easy it is to underestimate our gifts and miss our opportunities.

That Sunday morning in North Carolina I answered the cab driver, "Actually, I got the call as a child. I was four." He said, "To get the call as a child is a special privilege. God bless you."

Yes, I had wanted to be a rabbi as long as I could remember wanting to be anything. But somehow the call got placed on hold or the reception wasn't very good. Now I was carving out my path as a rabbi in a whole new way. Experimenting, taking risks, improvising my way without fear.

Now, instead of running, I was starting to listen.

forty-two

The Sabbath is a taste of the world to come.
THE TALMUD BERACHOT 57B

WHEN SHE walked through the door I barely recognized Michelle. It had been only two years since I'd last seen her, but she seemed to have aged by more than ten years. Her light brown hair looked frizzy and dull. I could see the white roots growing in her part. She had gained quite a bit of weight. Her face was lined and drawn. She was dressed in sweats. Through her tears she told me that she and her husband, Mitch, were losing the ability to reach their son, Adam. Adam was fifteen and Michelle described him as a teenager who had withdrawn inside himself and inside his room. She told me Adam would come home from school, grunt a hello at her, and run into his room. He'd come out to grab food from the fridge and then she wouldn't see him again until he left for school the following morning. When she'd try to enter his room, he'd tell her to get out. When she'd ask him about his day, he'd mumble something beneath his breath and walk away.

I tried to picture this boy I had known at his Bar Mitzvah, a boy with big blue eyes, so full of joy and so full of questions. Perhaps Adam had become a dark soul, or perhaps he was doing what all healthy teenagers do; he was carving out his own identity. When I asked Michelle what Adam was like at the dinner table, she said without missing a beat, "We don't eat together." Mitch worked long hours at the office and often ate dinner over meetings. Michelle ordered lots of takeout and ate alone at the kitchen table. Adam always ate in his bedroom in front of his computer.

She said to me, "Naomi, I'm losing him. Do you have any Jewish wisdom to help me get him back?" I thought for a moment, I thought about what it was that had kept my family together as we worried over Noa and as we watched her struggle to gain strength. I thought about what we were doing even on that ominous night when Dr. Becket called with Noa's test results.

I said to Michelle, "Shabbat."

She looked puzzled. She and Mitch had sent Adam to Hebrew school, he'd had a Bar Mitzvah, but that's about as far as their religious observance went.

I said to Michelle, "Shabbat is your opportunity to do it all differently."

I told her most people think of the Sabbath as a day of prohibition—you can't do this and you can't do that. But it's actually a day of permission, a day when we give ourselves permission to leave the workweek and all its demands behind so that we can breathe again, dream again, connect again. I wasn't advising her to suddenly observe the Jewish Sabbath in all its details, I was encouraging her to experience the blessings Shabbat might offer her.

We talked about what Friday night could look like in her home. We talked about turning off electronics—the computer, the TV, the cell phone, the iPod—and what a challenge that would be. And what a relief that would be. We talked about a home-cooked meal, about a return to the family table. We talked about having a conversation with Adam across a table set with a white tablecloth and flowers. We talked about candles and blessings and time. Time. Time passes much more slowly when you have nowhere to go and nothing to turn on. We talked about inviting guests. We also talked about her marriage and about Shabbat as an opportunity for rekindling romance.

Michelle left my study without making any promises to actually follow through on Shabbat. She said she was going to think about it. I wondered if she would.

Three weeks later, Michelle came to see me. There were tears streaming down her bright smiling face. She looked like a different woman, years younger. Her face was less worn and less lined. Her hair was shiny and blown dry. She was wearing a royal blue sweater set. "He's leaving his door open," she said to me. What a powerful metaphor. She told me about Shabbat and how they had invited over another family with a teenage girl. Not a bad idea. She told me about the meal she had made. She told me that since that Shabbat meal, she, Mitch, and Adam had begun to have dinner together almost every weeknight. She blushed and told me what a difference a little sex makes to a marriage.

When Michelle left, I started writing to myself, *During the weekdays we journey on in the desert. Our days can be long and trying. Life can spin out of control. But there is an oasis waiting for us just up ahead. A place of nourishment and peace where we can rest and take pleasure in beauty and blessings. It's not a solitary place, not a place to go to be alone, it's a place where weary travelers come to rest together and enjoy one another. The rabbis called the Sabbath a taste of heaven on earth. A time when we can get a glimpse of the world as we'd like it to be.*

The miracle of Shabbat is that its light spills over into the week and lights up our gray, harried days. The days leading up to Shabbat are illuminated with anticipation. The days following Shabbat shine in its afterglow. Suddenly we can see in living color again. We are no longer wandering aimlessly. Life has its pattern, its rhythm, its meaning.

forty-three

The heart is half a prophet.

YIDDISH PROVERB

I WAS sitting in my study waiting for Josh and Nicole to arrive. I had no idea what they wanted to discuss with me. While I waited I was making up a guest list for Noa's ninth birthday party. It was February 2005. Noa was all legs—slender and lovely. Now she seemed less like a drunken sailor and more like a fawn trying to find her legs. Watching her amble through a grassy field, she reminded me of Bambi first learning to walk. Noa was a beautiful creature with flowing golden curls. Because of her lean, long line she seemed graceful even though her coordination was quite poor. Quite often people who met her would ask me if she was a dancer.

She was getting stronger and stronger. She was even able to make it down a flight of stairs now with relative ease.

While I was scribbling down the names of Noa's friends, Josh and Nicole knocked on my study door. Now they were sitting on a couch opposite me, looking shell-shocked. I asked what the matter was. I was wondering if they might be having marital troubles. No, it was worse. I could tell. They were trying to be strong, struggling to hold it together. Nicole couldn't speak. I was trying to be of help in any way I could. Josh told me Ellie, their beautiful two-year-old little girl, had just been diagnosed with a fatal degenerative disease. My heart started pounding so hard I could hear it throbbing in my head. My throat was tight, my lungs were burning. Nicole's face was contorted in pain, Josh was pale and stoical. What words of wisdom did I have for them? What could I say? This same dark cloud had been hanging over my head for quite some time. It stopped me in my tracks. What to say? This was too close.

Nicole talked through her tears. She told me she didn't know how to carry on, how to act normal, how to wait for the terrible time when this would all play out. How could she take Ellie to school in the morning or invite her healthy bratty little girlfriends over with their happy, mindless mothers?

My mouth opened and words started coming out. I didn't know where the words were coming from. "How does Ellie look today?" I asked. They both responded, "Great." "Is Ellie happy today?" They both nodded, "Yes." "Here is what I think. We're living in a time of great scientific progress. But some of the knowledge has the power to rob us of amazingly precious times today. It's like looking into a crystal ball. If you were raising Ellie one hundred years ago, would you be in here in tears right now? No. You'd be picnicking in a park somewhere, raising her in perfect ignorant bliss. I'm not saying we should ignore science; every day brings with it the possibility of a new discovery, a new treatment, a new cure. I'm saying look at your child today and treasure all the good days you're having right now." Nicole was nodding her head; Josh was rocking back and forth taking it in. "Every day, look at Ellie and ask yourself: *How is Ellie today?* If she's healthy and she's happy, have a blast with her; try not to spend the time crying. Invite her bratty little girlfriends over, invite their blessed mindless mothers over too." The three of us started laughing. Laughing and crying.

I realized I was counseling myself. I was talking to me: *I've got my eyes open. No more standing on the dock. I've got to dive into life, I've got to enjoy every single precious day. I've got to enjoy every moment with my kids, every moment with Rob. I've got to stop taking time for granted. It's slipping away.*

forty-four

If you can't go over, you must go under.
YIDDISH PROVERB

NOA WAS seated between Rob and me on the plane. "So who are we seeing?" she asked. We told her we were going to see a doctor who would help her with her learning. It had taken me a whole year of weekly phone calls to get this appointment with Erica's brain guru.

Noa was excited to be traveling alone with the two of us. It wasn't often that she got me and Rob to herself. She was in heaven. We checked into our hotel, ate dinner out, got Noa ready for bed with her usual night rituals: the moon in the ocean, "Red River Valley," the Shema. She'd packed seven Beanie Babies to sleep with. She lay in bed surrounded by her zoo and fell sound asleep.

In the morning we had breakfast in the hotel and I could see Noa was having a bad day. She was wobbly and woozy, having trouble directing the spoonfuls of cereal into her mouth. When we were done eating and the waitress was clearing the table, Noa suddenly leaned over her cereal bowl and vomited her whole breakfast into it.

I thought the waitress was going to vomit too. But she kindly picked up Noa's bowl and told her, "You feel better soon, princess."

How were we supposed to have an evaluation with Noa feeling sick? We'd flown across the country, and now what? We went to the learning center and hoped for the best. We waited behind a two-way mirror and watched Noa's assessment. It took a lot of restraint not to shout out the answers to her. I wanted her to excel. I wanted to show Dr. Lapp and Dr. Lowe a thing or two.

After the morning tests, we met with the brain guru. Dr. Bloom tested Noa personally now. And then he sat us all down on the couch and explained his findings. He emphasized that it was important for Noa to hear what he had to say. He said too often kids with learning disabilities walk around feeling stupid or lazy because nobody ever told them how bright they are despite their deficits.

He turned to Noa and said, "You are really smart. You're good at understanding words and stories. You're perceptive and you have lots of good language skills. And you've also got areas in your brain that aren't working so well. Your biggest problem is memory. You've got problems remembering things. That's not the end of the world, but it means you need to learn how to take really good notes and remind yourself of things. And you're probably never going to be good at math. That's the truth. Math is always going to trip you up. But everyone has something they're not good at." He then added, "And you need to go to a school for kids with learning disabilities. You need to have teachers who are trained to teach you how to learn." Noa took all this in; she nodded. Then the doctor asked, "What did I say? Are you smart or stupid, Noa?" She answered, "I'm smart." "Yes, you're very smart and you need to go to a school that can help you get ahead."

Then Dr. Bloom turned to Rob and me and told us he had great faith in Noa's future learning. I was wondering if he had equal faith in her health, but I held my tongue.

In the cab on the way back to the airport, Noa just broke down. She was sobbing. Noa rarely cried. She was always so upbeat and positive. It broke my heart to see her so sad. I stroked her hair. "What's upsetting you?" I asked. She said, "I don't want to leave my school. I'm going to miss Amanda so much. You don't know how much fun recess is with her." I tried to paint for her a picture of a new school and new friends, but then I realized it wasn't time to cheer her up. She deserved a good cry. I said, "It hurts to leave a place you love." And I just held her as she wept.

After we put Noa to bed that night, Rob and I had a good cry of our own. We weren't quite ready to face the truth: Noa would not be able to magically catch up to her friends at school. We held each other and tried to remember the brain guru's promise: He had great hopes for Noa's future learning.

forty-five

If we cannot do what we will,
we must will what we can.
Yiddish proverb

THE NEXT day I began a search for the perfect school for Noa. This was no simple matter. First we had to petition the school district. This didn't go so well. In the end, the district refused to offer us funding for a special education school for Noa. Now we'd have to figure out how to pay for Noa's new school out of pocket.

We visited four schools and decided along with Noa that our first choice was a school called Park Century. It was a small school not far from our home with about ten children per class and a teacher and an aide in every class. Every child also had a private reading tutor and a private math tutor. I knew Noa wouldn't fall through the cracks there. I knew she'd get loads of help and personal attention. Tuition was going to be a stretch. We refinanced our home.

When I was lying in bed with Noa on the night before her very first day of school, she began to cry. She said, "I won't be able to pray at Park Century. It's not a Jewish school." I promised her, "We'll pray in the morning. We'll pray at home and we'll pray and sing in the car all the way to school."

And we did.

We gave thanks for waking up, for standing tall, for the new day. We sang and hoped and Noa hopped out of the car.

When I picked her up at the end of the day, she was all smiles. She said, "I think I'm going to like it here." And she did.

Day by day Noa was learning to take notes, learning to think on her own, learning to read on her own. In math? Well . . . she was doing her best.

forty-six

For the place on which you stand is holy ground.
Exodus 3:5

IT WAS spring break and Rob, Adi, Noa, and I were hiking in the Grand Canyon. Adi was running and climbing with a huge smile on his face. I was walking behind Rob, watching how he was hovering close to Noa making sure she didn't fall. Noa was standing on her own two feet, not falling over and not collapsing. Usually whenever we went hiking in LA, Rob inevitably ended up carrying Noa on his back. Her stamina was poor; her muscles would just give out. The Grand Canyon offered far more challenging terrain than Noa had ever attempted. It was steep and the altitude didn't help matters any. But there she was, laughing and singing and slowly making her way.

I'd never seen the Grand Canyon before. There I was face-to-face with this spectacular sight. I can't even put the feelings I had there into coherent sentences. Words come up, though: awe, timelessness, beauty, grandeur, God.

Everything was in perfect perspective. My smallness, eternity's greatness, nature's wonder, God's hand. And Noa hiked without needing to be carried.

We got home on a Sunday night. I felt replenished and solid. And then on Monday morning I bit into a piece of toast and a filling fell out of my tooth. My mom called a moment later to tell me she'd taken a bad fall and was in the hospital. With the phone to my ear, I walked into the kitchen and I saw water pouring out of the pipe below the sink. Noa started calling for me from her room: Her toilet was overflowing. Next, I went on the Internet and saw that Nashuva had lost its Web site. I made many phone calls until I learned that somehow our domain name had lapsed. We didn't own our name in cyberspace in perpetuity. Nashuva just disappeared.

All that in one day. Just twelve hours earlier, I had been standing before the Grand Canyon; everything was in perfect perspective.

I started thinking about Michelle and how quickly life can spin out of control. Daily life can paralyze and blind us. It took no time at all before I found myself overwhelmed by my own whirlwind.

Later that night, after the plumber left, I sat down, breathed a sigh of relief, and wrote in my journal:

It's so much easier to be holy on a mountaintop than it is to be holy in the daily grind of life, in the little and not so little crises of life.

But now I understand that's what holiness is all about. We don't need to be holy by secluding ourselves in a cave or on a mountaintop.

I thought about what the Bible said about how to live a holy life. It asked us to be holy by living in *this* world. It asked us to honor our parents, to care for the weak, to love one another, to be honest in business, to be compassionate to animals.

That's what being holy meant.

I wrote on, *Yes an ordinary day is filled with all sorts of setbacks and* challenges and confrontations and disappointments. We can let these setbacks stop us in our tracks. We can allow them to shake us. Or we can see them as opportunities for living a holy life.

It's so much easier to find holiness in life's highs. It was easier for the Children of Israel to find holiness in the Exodus, in the face of miracles, of seas parting, than it was to find holiness in the schlep, in the journey out of Egypt through the desert in the heat without shade or food.

But that's our challenge. To find holiness in each day.

It's so much easier to find holiness in the ideal of God, the loving, all-powerful, omniscient God of the universe who never slumbers or sleeps, than it is to find holiness in a God who is silent in the face of suffering and death and disease and terror and war and genocide and natural disaster.

But that's our challenge. To find holiness and faith in this broken, breathtaking world.

Just then I thought about a scene from *The Graduate*, one of my favorite movies of all time. There are a lot of great hysterical moments in that movie, but the most powerful to me is that last shot when you see their frightened faces as they're sitting there in the back of that bus.

I wrote to myself, *Life is what happens after they get off that bus.*

Hope Will Find You

forty-seven

If I try to be like him, who will be like me?
YIDDISH PROVERB

"CAW-CAW-CAW!" A strange sound woke me out of my sleep. It was 5:00 a.m. Noa was calling for Rob. Rob was walking around the house looking utterly confused. Adi was sleeping through this racket.

I was traveling quite a bit giving lectures around the country at that time. Rob had a running game he liked to play with me. Every time I left home to give a lecture, he did something unexpected. In December 2006, I came home to three chickens. We named them Empira (in honor of Empire Kosher chicken), Colonel Sanders, and Kojak. Kojak got her name when our second dog, Kira, attacked her and pulled all the feathers from the top of her head.

When I returned from a weekend away in May 2007, there was a little chick in my backyard going, "Peep." It was my neighbor's daughter's Easter chick. Knowing we already had three chickens, she asked Rob if we would take it. My kids named her Fluffy.

Well, Fluffy grew and her feathers turned from yellow fuzz to auburn. The other hens were mean to her. They wouldn't let her in the coop, so she started sleeping on the fence.

Although we kept calling Fluffy a girl, one question remained: Was Fluffy a girl or a boy? With chicks only an expert could tell.

I started to call Fluffy "Pat" after that ambiguously gendered character from *Saturday Night Live*. We all waited to see what Fluffy would become, and Fluffy continued to sit on the fence. Literally and figuratively.

Two weeks passed, and Rob found a fourth egg in the nest. He announced, "Fluffy's a girl!"

But now that faint "Caw-caw-CAW" that woke me out of my sleep was getting louder, "CAW-CAW-CAW!" Noa thought Rob was playing some sort of trick on her. She yelled out from her bedroom, "Daddy, stop that, I'm sleeping." He hollered back, "It's not me."

Fluffy was a dude. And suddenly those hens who were so mean to Fluffy couldn't get enough of him.

I'm a nice Jewish girl from Brooklyn and suddenly I was living in Green Acres with two dogs, three chickens, and a rooster.

The day Fluffy started to crow, Rob started to search on Craigslist for a new owner. There was a man named Alan who was on his way over when I intercepted him. I said to Rob, "I'm not ready to give Fluffy away. I know the neighbors are going to kill us, but give me just a few more days with Fluffy."

Why did I want to keep Fluffy a bit longer? Because, thinking like a rabbi, I knew there was a spiritual lesson I was supposed to learn from Fluffy; I needed time to figure out the message. And I loved hearing Fluffy crow in the morning. I was addicted to it. I'd race out of bed to watch him spread his wings, arch his neck up to the first glimmer of light in a darkened sky, and offer up his call. Fluffy put me in harmony with nature. And that was no easy task.

So here is what Fluffy taught me: Stop sitting on the fence.

Reveal yourself, and those who ignored you will flock to you. Finding your way is not so much about choosing a direction, I realized. It's about uncovering the voice, the call that is already imprinted inside you, and then finding the courage to face down your fears and let your true voice be heard.

All those months Fluffy was trying to be a chicken and it wasn't working out. All those nights sitting all alone on the fence. Then his voice came to him, and Fluffy became the master of the coop.

One of my favorite verses from the Song of Songs is when the lover calls out: "Let me hear your voice, for your voice is sweet." The ancient rabbis insisted it was God who was speaking those words to each one of us, "Let me hear your voice, for your voice is sweet."

It takes time and courage to find your voice. I knew this. We spend so much time in life trying to imitate other people or trying to live up to the projections people put on us. Or the projections we put on ourselves. Sometimes people expect too much from us and we become paralyzed with fear. Sometimes they expect too little from us and we believe them.

About two months after Fluffy found his voice, I was cleaning out Noa's backpack at the end of her school year and I found a spiral notebook full of entries she had written. I aimlessly flipped through the pages and then I read one entry. I couldn't believe Noa had written this. Where did it come from? That voice of hers. That depth. I slid down on the floor of her bedroom and read on. My tears were dripping on her words. The handwriting was barely legible, but the words were full of wisdom and encouragement. To whom was Noa talking in her writings? Did she know she was talking to me? I started thinking about Dr. Lapp and Dr. Lowe and all their dark prophecies. Noa had other plans for herself. Her concise, optimistic teachings reminded me of Yoda; again I repeated to myself, "The force is strong with this one."

When she got home and I asked Noa about the pieces she'd written, she shrugged them off as if to say, "No big deal." When I asked for her permission to share them with others, she smiled and said, "Sure." I call them, "Noa's Twelve Rules for Living a Rich Life."

1. Be Adventurous

You can sit at home and be grumpy and life will mean nothing to you. Or you can go on an adventure through life and try stuff you never thought you would do, and life will be exciting for you. You shouldn't just sit around and do nothing, because there should be some pretty cool adventures in life.

2. Be Kind to Yourself

If you're mean to yourself, others will be mean to you. So respect yourself. It's a good thing. People will see your positive outlook and add to your happiness.

3. Make Mistakes

If you don't do anything you will never make a mistake. If you don't make a mistake you will never try anything. So make mistakes; it will be good in the end.

4. Laugh

When you are in a bad mood and someone makes you laugh, it gives you a jump start to your day. My friend once hurt her head and I said something funny and made her laugh and then that really cheered her up. So always try to laugh even in a bad situation and it will make your day.

5. Lift Your Own Spirits

If you are sad or down you have to will yourself not to be down anymore. One morning, I was driving in the car to school, and I said to myself, "I don't have any talent," and I got really sad. Then I thought, "I can blow the Shofar," which is a Jewish instrument. After I thought of that, my sadness went away. So remember you can wish yourself up.

6. Play to Your Strengths

If you can do something, don't let it get involved with what you can't do. I can't do math so well, but I can do reading really well if I try. So I don't get my good reading mixed up with my bad math. So don't let your good get mixed up with your bad.

7. Ask Yourself for Help

If you are having trouble with something, think first before you ask someone for help. Once, my mom was having trouble writing a sermon. Before she asked anybody for help she thought about it some more and wrote a great sermon. So think before you ask for help. It will be better.

8. Live Up to Your Dreams

If you have dreams they're probably not going to happen if you don't live up to them. None of my dreams are going to happen if I don't stick with them and believe they're going to happen. So follow your dreams. What can go wrong? Most everything will come true.

201

9. Be a Friend

Nobody is ever perfect, so your friends have to learn to look past your faults. I make lots of mistakes and my best friend needs to learn how to ignore my faults. Someone isn't going to like you because you know everything. They're going to like you because you truly can care. My best friend wants to be with me even if she doesn't like the same things I like. True friends are the people who really care for you when you need them.

10. Don't Let Mean People Shake You

If someone is being mean to you, it's probably because they have emotional problems. At my old school there was this girl and she was always mean to me and talked about me behind my back. That mean girl said I was so weak. She said I couldn't do anything. Now, I wasn't going to sit there and take her rudeness. I went out there and proved that I could do it. You can do anything you want to do. Don't let some negativity hold you back.

11. Forgive

If someone hurts your feelings, you will be offended, but it can be fixed. Although it will be fixed, it may still hurt. I once had a big fight with my friend at school. She was yelling very loudly and I didn't know what to say. My throat was clogged up and I was crying. And she was crying too. We finally made up and became good friends in the end. You know you can't change the past, but you can change the future.

12. Stand Up to Peer Pressure

You know who you are. You don't need anyone to tell you who you are. I know I should just keep living life the way I do. I'm strong. I don't have to do whatever other people tell me I should do. Be strong! Be smart! Make good decisions!

The bald man in the waiting room had promised me, "She is something special. She's got the real thing, that rare quality." And she did. Evalina had told me, "This girl is tough." And she was. Noa had a powerful voice. In her writing she was already talking to an audience.

"Let me hear your voice, for your voice is sweet."

forty-eight

The longer a blind man lives, the more he sees.
YIDDISH PROVERB

EVALINA WAS right, Noa *was* tough. All of a sudden I found myself thinking back on all the therapists and specialists who had
worked with Noa over the years.

The truth is, some of them weren't very impressive.

There was Jennie the occupational therapist, who always seemed
miserable and bored out of her head. She sounded just like Eeyore.
She'd whine, "Hi, Noa, come with me." And then I'd watch her sit
there at the table beside Noa with her chin in her hand as she kept
yawning and yawning.

Then there was Ilene the physical therapist, who was scared of
Noa. Every day she'd bring Noa into the gym and say, "Hey, Noa, do
you want to climb today?" And Noa would say, "No," and Ilene wouldn't
know what to do. Then a lightbulb would go off in her head and she'd
say, "Hey, Noa, do you want to catch today?" And Noa would say, "No,"
and just sit there on the bench. That's how the whole hour of therapy
would pass.

And I'd ask myself, "Am I really paying money for this?"

Finally I talked to Ilene and said, "If you want Noa to do something, why are you asking her permission? Do you think I say to Noa, 'Hey, Noa, do you want to brush your teeth today?'"

Some of Noa's therapists seemed to hate kids.

One doctor reminded me of Krusty the Clown from the *Simpsons* cartoon, "Here, kid, take a lollipop . . . Now get lost!"

When she was around six years old we noticed Noa was having problems with visual perception. She had perfect vision, but she couldn't see things. She couldn't see a ball coming at her and be ready to catch it. She couldn't understand how to put a puzzle together.

Eeyore suggested we go see a vision therapist named Dr. Bill Takeshita.

Given our experience with Noa's other therapists, I didn't exactly have high hopes for Dr. Takeshita, but just the same I took Noa to see him.

The waiting room was full of children with all sorts of disabilities, and then Dr. Takeshita walked in and all the kids started screaming, "Dr. Bill, Dr. Bill!"

This man was the Pied Piper if there ever was one.

Then it was Noa's turn to see Dr. Bill. He was a gift from God. In no time at all he was able to understand the world as Noa saw it.

He had all sorts of contraptions in his office, some of which he had designed himself, all to help kids begin to read the world they saw.

He was working on Noa's hand-eye coordination, on her tracking pictures across a page. He was showing her how every little piece of a puzzle was related to all the other pieces and how the pieces all fit together into a bigger whole.

Week after week we'd go back to see Dr. Bill and week after week Noa's world was getting wider and wider.

During the appointments I'd sit off in a corner and watch Dr. Takeshita at work. He struck me as one of those rare people who was living his bliss. What a gift.

In December of that year we went back east for Chanukah, and when we returned in January for our usual appointment, we walked through the door and parents in the waiting room were crying.

I walked up to the receptionist, "Where's Dr. Bill?" She was fighting back tears and she said, "Dr. Bill has retired."

"He's forty-two years old. What do you mean he's retired?"

The receptionist said, "He's lost his vision."

"What? In two weeks?"

"Yes, he's going blind."

Now I started crying. How was that possible? What cruel irony.

We never saw Dr. Takeshita again. Six years passed, but I often thought about him. I wondered what happened to him. Did his life fall apart? Did he become angry or bitter? That man was born to be an eye doctor. Did he find a new career? Did he feel useless? I wondered if he was happy.

One day when I was flooded with thoughts about Dr. Takeshita, I wrote: *Sometimes doors close on us. Someone broke up with you. Your business failed. Someone fired you. Your child went off to college. A loved one died. You're never going to have a biological child.*

And sometimes we spend our lives banging on the locked door behind us.

For some of us that door closed a long time ago and we've been in too much denial to notice it.

We can keep banging on the closed door or we can turn around and no-tice the new room we're in. When we turn around, we may discover, "It's not a room at all! It's an expanse, a new vista, a new space."

It's no accident that so many biblical stories are about this exact subject: people who have perfect vision but they can't see what's in front of them or what's around them.

Abraham thinks he's supposed to sacrifice his son Isaac and he's so busy tying up his son that he can't see there's a ram caught in the thicket right in front of him.

*I think the Bible repeats this theme over and over again to teach us that a life of blessings **is a matter of visual perception.***

What are you focusing on and what's the bigger picture you're missing?

In the summer between sixth and seventh grades, Noa's teacher gave her a summer reading list. And Noa was having a really hard time getting through the books she was supposed to read.

She'd read the same page over and over again and wasn't getting anywhere. Then I thought it might be easier for her to listen to the books on tape. She's a really good listener. So I downloaded them for her on iTunes and she listened to them as she followed along in the book. What a difference the audiobooks made. She devoured two books in three days.

When I was telling a friend of mine about this new discovery, she told me that her daughter who was in college had a minor learn-ing disability and the school's learning center was able to get all her textbooks on tape for her from the Braille Institute. And she told me I should look into this for Noa.

So I Googled "free audiobooks" and I came upon a center in LA where I could find all sorts of them. I called the center and asked what they had available for Noa and the woman on the phone said, "There's one person who knows everything there is to know about this and I'll have him get back to you."

The next day my phone rang, I picked it up, and who was on the line? Dr. Bill Takeshita!

He said to me, "Wait a minute, your name is Naomi Levy. Are you a rabbi?" I said, "Yes, that's me!" He wanted to hear all about how Noa was doing. He couldn't believe she was already entering seventh grade.

And then with the patience and wisdom I had come to know and respect, he carefully explained to me all of Noa's options in the world of audiobooks.

I thanked him. We hung up.

Then I called back. I told him what an inspiration he was to me and to so many and I wanted to understand his story. I wanted to know what had happened to him.

And he told me.

By the time he was forty-two he had everything he'd ever dreamed of. He was happily married with a wife and two amazing kids. He loved his work. When a friend would call and say, "Come play golf with me," he'd answer, "I already have a hobby. My hobby is working with these kids."

Dr. Bill was at the top of his profession. People would fly here from all over the world just so he could see their kids. The sultan of Brunei, the governor, movie stars, famous athletes.

Then he started to notice a blind spot in his left eye. He ignored it. He thought he just needed some rest. But sure enough he found out it was a degenerative eye disease.

There was nothing he could do.

He would never be able to examine a child's eyes again. He had to leave his practice. And he told me he was devastated. He was so angry, so bitter. He got depressed. He just sat at home alone all day. He didn't want to see family. He didn't want to see his friends. He didn't want to go outside. He was so ashamed. He didn't want anyone to see he was blind. He was mean to his wife. He told me, "My wife might spend hours making a nice chicken dinner and I'd say, 'Why'd you make chicken? I don't want chicken.'"

He lost his faith in God.

He started to think about wanting to die. He said to himself, "If I'm dead my family will be happier without me. If I'm dead at least they'll get the insurance money."

So he started thinking about ways to kill himself.

And when Dr. Takeshita's life was at the very lowest low, his brother had a massive heart attack and lost 70 percent of his heart function. And Dr. Takeshita's brother's reaction to his situation was the complete opposite of his own.

His brother was so positive, so optimistic, so full of hope when his heart was so damaged that his only hope was to receive a heart transplant.

He asked his brother, "Why aren't you angry? Why aren't you bitter?" And his brother told him, "If I'm angry now it's only going to ruin my life now and I want to enjoy every precious day I've got."

Dr. Takeshita's brother died before he could get that transplant.

And suddenly his own problems seemed to melt away. Suddenly he began to see his life again.

He told me, "I was so focused on my retina, which is as small as a postage stamp, and I couldn't see I was wasting precious years."

He continued, "We all do this. We think about our own problems:

I'm blind, I'm deaf, I have an illness, I don't have enough money, I'm not a good athlete, I'm not a good student . . . And we can't see the good that's around us."

He realized he had so much knowledge to share as a blind eye doctor. He could use his personal experience to change the way doctors treat patients. In a very short span of time he had gone from being someone with perfect vision to someone who was totally blind, and he had a lot to say.

At first he took small steps back into his professional world.

He told me a major hurdle he had to overcome was, "How am I going to give lectures if I can't see my notes?" I asked him how he did it. He said he realized he could visualize his entire lecture. He could see the whole sequence in his mind. And he told me his lectures were more interesting now than they ever were when he was reading from a prepared script.

With Dr. Takeshita's talent, with his knowledge and his passion, it didn't take long before he became a major force in the field of low vision. He soon became an adjunct professor at the Southern California College of Optometry, the chief of optometry at the Center for the Partially Sighted, and the director of low vision at the Braille Institute.

He told me that in his spare time he offers two podcasts every week. One where he discusses all the latest technology for people with low vision. And one just for students with low vision where he inspires them to do their very best at school.

And he also hosts a national call-in show called *Ask Dr. Bill* where he helps people with low vision take full advantage of the world. He said the topic of his latest show was: "How do you use an iPhone if you're totally blind?"

When we came to the end of our conversation, I asked Dr. Takeshita, "Can you tell me what's the most important thing you've learned from your experience?"

And he said to me, "Rabbi, here's what I've learned: I used to think, 'These things don't happen to me.' But now I can see every person . . . we all go through difficulties. Every single person has some kind of weakness and that's okay. Because everybody has something. If you can acknowledge that you have a weakness, you will learn ways to adjust to it. The time when I tried to hide myself was the hardest thing of all. I didn't want to go out in public. I was almost paranoid. But then I learned it's not difficult to go outside. People are just curious when they see me with my cane. Now I can teach blind people how I've coped and gotten over it. Now I can tell a kid with dyslexia: 'You know what? I have a form of dyslexia too and it's called blindness and I read faster now than when I was able to see.'"

When I hung up with Dr. Bill I told myself: *Doors do close on us. And it isn't easy to let go. Some people lose money. Some lose their jobs. Some battle illness. We all lose loved ones.*

I thought of Noa. Yes, Noa has disabilities and it's unfair that she has so many challenges. Long ago I promised myself if she lived I'd never complain again. Yes, I wish there were no obstacles in her path, but there are. There always will be. Deal with it. She is dealing with it beautifully.

Sometimes we get so crushed by what we've lost that we forget what we have. We all have legitimate causes for feeling bitter, but we all want a sweet life.

With that door safely locked behind you, you can turn around to greet a new time of blessings.

Dr. Bill taught me that bitterness and sweetness aren't things that happen to us. They are choices we make.

For heaven's sake: Choose the sweetness.

forty-nine

And the city shall be rebuilt on its ruins.

JEREMIAH 30:18

I HEARD the doorbell ring. My friend Ed from the Nashuva band was standing at the front door. He had come to give Noa a piano lesson. By now Noa was in the seventh grade, with long dirty blond curls and wearing skinny jeans and Uggs.

I called out to Ed, "The door is stuck. Go around the back."

That fall the weather started to change a bit, as much as the weather ever changes in LA, and Rob and I noticed that our front door was starting to stick a little when we tried to open it. We thought it was moisture; after all, we live in Venice Beach. A few weeks later, we really had to push to get that door open. Rob and I kept saying, "We really need to call Walter to plane down the door." But we convinced ourselves that it was just a little warped from moisture and the problem would probably go away all by itself.

By January I had to use my hip to open the door. By February I actually had to take a running start and throw my whole body against the door to get it to open. And we kept saying, "We really need to get Walter here to plane down the door."

By March there was just no way to open our front door. No matter how hard we pushed, we could not get that front door open. So . . . we started to use the back door. We just gave up on our front door. Every day all four of us would go out through the back door and come home through the back door. When anyone would come to visit, they'd ring the bell at the front door and I'd meet them there, open the peephole, and shout, "Come around through the back door."

Then that night Ed came over to teach Noa. I met him at our back door. He came inside and we were sitting in the living room when he asked me, "So, Naomi, what's with the front door?" I said, "You know, it's moisture, the door's warped and we've got to get Walter the handyman over to plane it down."

Ed took a look at the door and then he looked around the room and said to me, "Naomi, it's not the door." I said, "What do you mean? Of course it's the door." He looked around the room again and saw I had a big blue Pilates ball. He took the ball, put it down in the middle of our living room, and told me, "Just watch this." On its own, the ball rolled right toward the front door. And he took the ball and put it somewhere else in the room and again, lo and behold, the ball rolled right toward the front door. He said to me, "Naomi, it's not the door, it's your house. Your whole house is falling down." We went out the back door and around the house to look at the outside of the front door and Ed showed me the cracks above the door and the cracks along the base of the wall. I said, "Oh, is that why we have those cracks?" Our house was falling down. The entire living room floor was on a slant.

Now we called Walter.

Walter crawled under our house and sure enough, our house was falling off the foundation. All the wooden beams holding our house up were rotted and crumbling, and in some areas there was only a foot of clearance between the house and the foundation below it.

That meant Walter could only bring in short, skinny men to do this work. If a worker was too tall or if he had a stomach at all, there was no way he could fit under the house. In short, Walter said, "I'll have to hire elves." I have to say it really did look like the casting call for *The Wizard of Oz*. All these petite guys kept showing up at our front door. They'd ring the bell and I could barely see them through the peephole. "Hello?" I'd call out. "Is anybody there?" I'd look way down and then, "Oh, hello."

First, they had to dig a tunnel under our house and remove all the dirt so they could have enough clearance to work there. Next, they had to jack up the whole front end of our house and start replacing all the rotted beams.

It was costing us thousands upon thousands of dollars. With that money we could have put in a whole new kitchen. With that money we could have remodeled our living room and our dining room and people would have said, "Ooh, aah." But we spent all that money and no one would ever be able to tell. All our money, every dollar went under the house to a place where no one would ever see it.

We spent all that money and we were left with nothing to show for it except for one thing: We had a front door that opened. And that in itself was a great miracle, wasn't it? Things got so much simpler in our household. We no longer had to push to get in; we didn't have to go around the back. All we had to do was turn the key and— poof—we were home.

I knew my rotting-foundation story was a metaphor for the way we all live in denial. I wrote the lesson down in my journal: *We all neglect problems in this way somewhere in our lives. You have a toothache and instead of going to the dentist right away, you think it's brilliant to just start chewing on the other side until it becomes a huge cavity.*

214

Every time we tell ourselves things will repair themselves, they get worse. Problems grow.

Eventually everything breaks. Things we once imagined were solid, they break too. Giant corporations break, glaciers break, promises break, resolutions break, dreams break, faith breaks, relationships break, hearts break too.

Yes, things will break. But I want to believe we have the power to repair what's broken. Things can be fixed, and the only way they will ever get fixed is through our own effort.

Of course, not everything can be repaired. Some things are just too broken to fix. Sometimes the best response is to demolish a building that's rotting and condemned. There are times we stay too long on a path that's crushing our spirits and we do need to carve out a new course.

But there are other times when we are tempted to give up on broken things that can still be saved. It takes one set of skills to build something new from the ground up, but it takes a whole different set of skills to repair something that's broken. That takes a certain kind of faith and gentleness.

I began thinking about a man named John whom I had counseled years before. John's parents came to this country with nothing and they built a very lucrative furniture business from the ground up. When John was just a kid, his dad would take him into the store and he'd say to him, "Johnnie, you'll never have to worry about money like I did when I was a kid. This will all be yours one day. This business will take care of you always." John never did have to worry. He went right into the family business. And he hated it. He told me he wasn't interested in sofas and he didn't know how to tell his dad he wanted to leave. How do you break your father's heart like that? So instead, John went to work every day and walked around resenting his father for not understanding him.

I was counseling John and I said to him, "John, honestly, you don't have the right to resent your father for not understanding you if you've never even told him how you're feeling." John responded, "Rabbi, you don't know my father. He's a difficult man." One day John finally gathered up the courage and the nerve to talk to his father. He told him, "Dad, I'm not happy here. It's killing me here. I've got to leave." And his difficult father said, "Johnnie, what took you so long?" And they both just hugged each other and wept.

As I reflected on John, I wrote to myself: *People can surprise us. We can surprise them. And we can even surprise ourselves.*

But there's someone we can't surprise. God. Because whatever we've been dreaming for ourselves doesn't even begin to scratch the surface of the potential God has already placed inside us. As big as our dreams are, God's dreams for us are even bigger. No matter how broken our lives may be, no matter how far we've strayed, no matter how long we've procrastinated, God is here to show us the way home through the front door.

Maybe we've been assuming the door is stuck when the whole foundation is falling down. Some people get to that truth the hard way through life-threatening illness. Some of us are lucky to get to that truth by arriving at a moment of clarity. The truth is we're careless with life. We walk around with this illusion of certainty, but everything is uncertain and temporary and fragile. How much of our short time on earth do we want to spend ignoring problems?

As I sat there writing these thoughts down in my journal about the way we all deny problems, I knew there was something I was ignoring that was eating away at me.

The truth? What was I ignoring? Noa's Bat Mitzvah.

fifty

For the mountains may crumble, and the hills may shake;
but My love will never leave you.

ISAIAH 54:10

ON THE bookshelf right beside the door to my bedroom, I kept passing by the big red book my father had used to teach me for my Bat Mitzvah. I treasured this book. It was my most precious inheritance from my father.

I knew it was time to start teaching Noa for her Bat Mitzvah. She was almost twelve.

Two years earlier I had taught Adi for his Bar Mitzvah from this same book. It was such a joy and an honor to be able to teach him all that my father had taught me.

And now it was Noa's turn to learn, but I was too scared to teach her. Every time I passed that red book I'd try to avert my gaze as if I could feel its eyes on me, saying, "So, what are you waiting for?" Noa and I were both engaged in a denial dance. Every now and then I'd ask her halfheartedly if she wanted to study with me and she'd say no. And every now and then she'd bring up the subject of her Bat Mitzvah and ask if she could do some sort of abbreviated service and I'd say no.

Why was I so scared to teach Noa for her Bat Mitzvah? I was afraid that because of her learning disabilities she wouldn't be able to learn her Torah and Haftorah portions. It was a lot to learn. It involved mastering the Hebrew reading and learning how to sight-read the cantillation signs. These are the musical notations that appear on every word of the text. And there were two different sets of cantillations to learn—one for the Torah reading and one for the Haftorah. And there were prayers to learn. And then we'd be studying the meaning of her Torah portion and she'd be writing and delivering her own sermon.

I was afraid because I wasn't sure I knew how to teach Noa and I wasn't sure I knew how much to demand of her. I didn't want to place too heavy a burden on her and I didn't want to underestimate her abilities either. Also, I was afraid of feeling disappointed if Noa wasn't able to learn what I so eagerly wanted to teach her. So I did nothing.

And then one Friday morning, I was studying Torah at Starbucks with Toba, my Chevrutah, and she said to me, "Listen to me, Noa is more capable than you know. Start teaching her and you'll see."

So that night I crawled into bed with Noa and we began learning together. Every night we'd crawl into bed together and learn. I was so mistaken. Noa was soaking up her studies with such passion. It wasn't easy, though. Together we had to devise our own way of learning the cantillations. First I taught her by drawing with my finger across her palm. Then we began to use all sorts of hand motions. I also color-coded all the musical signs. Noa astounded me. She mastered her blessings and the two types of cantillation in no time at all. Before long she knew her portion well enough to read it straight from the Torah scroll itself, which requires an enormous amount of memorization since the Torah has no vowels, no punctuation, and no cantillation marks in it. Some nights I was too tired to teach and I'd tell Noa to just go to bed, but she wouldn't hear of it. She'd fluff up a pillow for me and say, "Get in right now and start teaching me." Every night became a sacred experience.

And then we studied her Haftorah. It was a prophecy of hope from the Book of Isaiah. I asked Noa to tell me what the Haftorah meant to her. She spoke and I wrote:

I think it means, if someone doesn't have good luck, if you're missing something, you will find it, so don't lose hope in yourself. Someone might bring you down, or you might get sad, but don't worry, because God will be with you and will make you happy. Don't think someone else is luckier than you, because you will become luckier than those who are already lucky.

If you don't feel happy, just wait, because you are going to be very happy soon. Just wait, because your life is going to be bigger and more filled with joy. Someone will always be with you even though the world may change and so many things may happen. You will always have God with you no matter what.

Maybe God is telling us that if you don't like your life, if you really try to enjoy life, you will find hope. No . . . hope will find you.

Sometimes I feel sad and start crying for no apparent reason. I think God is saying that someway I will find a way to be happy again. I just feel when I look at people who don't have disabilities, who are really put together, I feel sad that I'm not that person. But then I realize that I'm special in my own way and no one else can compare to me. I have a life that no one else can ever have because I'm my own person and I live my own life.

Toba said, "Noa is more capable than you know. Start teaching her and you'll see." The bald angel said, "She is something special."

Noa said, "Hope will find you."

I gasped when Noa said, "Hope will find you." I'd been trying to hold on to hope for so long, to grasp at every little sign of improvement, of good news, like it was the happy end of this long wait. I'd spent so much time searching for hope. But my child was telling me I didn't need to push so hard or to hang on so desperately. Noa was telling me to relax and let hope in, like a kind of grace. "Hope will find you" sounded familiar to me, like an ancient biblical verse, even though this was the first time I'd ever heard it put that way. It reminded me of the Twenty-third Psalm, "Surely goodness and mercy will follow me all the days of my life." Noa was saying hope would follow me too.

Be Bold

fifty-one

*Open for me the gates of justice, I will enter them
and praise God.*

PSALM 118:19

THE BELLHOP led me and Noa into our room. I was expecting
two queen beds, but instead we'd gotten a single king. The new
sleeping arrangement felt right. We'd have a real slumber party, just
us girls.

In December I was invited to participate in a panel discussion in
Washington, D.C., and I'd invited Noa to join me on this trip. We
unpacked our bags, ate the chocolates off the pillows, and set out to
see the sights. We had such a magical time together. During the days
we visited the monuments and the museums. On our final day we
went to the Museum of American History and saw Dorothy's ruby
slippers and Jerry Seinfeld's puffy shirt. And then we came upon the
exhibit that contained the original Woolworth's counter where four
African American students had staged the famous sit-ins in Greens-
boro, North Carolina. Noa sat riveted. She was so inspired by the
courage of those four students and all the others who joined them in
protest.

At night we snuggled in our king-size bed and sang the song we learned that day at the Woolworth's counter exhibit. "I'm on my way to Freedom Land." And then I let her watch the movie *Wedding Crashers* as long as she agreed to let me cover her eyes during the sexy parts.

On the day of the panel discussion, the interviewer asked a group of women leaders to answer this question: "For a moment, imagine yourself in high school. Get a good mental image of that girl, her hopes and fears, interests and aspirations. What do you know now that you wish you could tell her? What would she think of the person you've become?"

I couldn't believe anyone saw me as a leader. I felt like an imposter.

I was scared to answer the question. When I thought about myself, I judged myself as a person who had been stalled and was just beginning to get back on track. But then I thought about her, about that teenage girl and what she would have thought of me. And I suddenly realized just how far I had already come. I suddenly could see my childhood dreams, I could see how I had held them close despite all sorts of obstacles. I suddenly could see that I had the power to keep living my dreams. I looked out at the packed audience, then I focused on a single empty seat in the front row. I pictured my teenage self in that seat and slowly I began to speak to her:

> I knew I wanted to be a rabbi from a very young age. But when I was in high school I was in an Orthodox yeshiva that scorned the very idea of women rabbis. Inside I wanted to be a rabbi and I couldn't even announce that, I couldn't even say that out loud. I was so ashamed of wanting to be a rabbi.
>
> I wanted to be a rabbi, but the Conservative rabbinical

seminary wasn't admitting women, so I had this secret fantasy that could never be . . .

And at that same time in my life, my father was murdered in a street mugging. So all the faith I had was in turmoil. I had so many struggles with God. Where was the God I had believed in so deeply and so passionately? What happened to that joyous faith that made me want to be a rabbi? How could I make sense of all of that?

And now I'm looking at that girl, the girl with the dreams and the shame and the pain and all those closed doors. I can see her in that seat in front of me. And it blows my mind because I can say to her: "You'll heal. Trust me, horrible things happen and you'll heal. And not only will you heal, but the pain you experienced will give you the strength to help other people. And all that shame about wanting to be a rabbi in this environment you're in where people don't accept you, where you can never even admit that you want to be a rabbi, that shame will turn into pride. Trust me, one day you'll be a rabbi. A Conservative rabbi. Doors will open."

That's what I would say to her, that's what I would say to all of us. Doors open that you would never imagine could open. You can heal, you can overcome. And when the opening comes, seize that opening. Take it and do with it whatever you will. Because doors open when you least expect it. And your life can open up before you in ways that you never imagined.

Not such a shabby answer.

Of course, I wasn't just talking to my fifteen-year-old self, I was talking to the adult who had somehow forgotten these important words of hope and encouragement. Doors were opening for me and they were opening for Noa despite all her challenges.

That night I lay in our hotel bed wide awake watching Noa sleep. I remembered the night of Dr. Becket's call and how I had crawled into bed with her and wept. She was so small back then in her footsie pj's. Now all sprawled out in slumber she took up three-quarters of the bed. Noa's doctors told us we'd have to wait seven years to tell whether she had A-T or not. Well, those seven long years of waiting were almost over. I had noticed myself breathing more deeply lately. Noa was growing stronger and stronger. As the noose finally began to lift from around her neck, I found myself thinking back on just how far Noa had come over the past seven years.

A memory of a snowy day in 2005 appeared before my eyes.•

fifty - two

The smoothest path is full of stones.
YIDDISH PROVERB

I WAS looking at Adi sitting there in the passenger seat of my car in his down jacket and gloves. He had graduated to the front seat that year. There was so much I wanted to explain to him.

It was the winter of 2005 and our family was on a ski trip. That night I took Adi out to the movies to see *King Kong*. We arrived at the theater quite early, and for a while we were sitting in the car watching the snow fall. It was getting dark out and the snow was coming down all around us. For some reason it felt like the right time to talk to Adi about Noa. I wanted to explain to him why he was taking his ski lessons in the main building when Noa was taking her lessons in the Adaptive Sports Center. I said, "Adi, Noa's muscles are a bit weak; that's how she was born."

Silence filled the air between us, the snow fell in silence all around us. And then Adi shot back, "No, Mom, you're wrong. Inside she's strong." Vapor smoke poured out of his mouth when he spoke these words. A mighty spirit of defiance.

* * *

Now it was January 2008. Noa was about to turn twelve. It was seven years since the night of that Sabbath meal when we received that fateful phone call. Seven years. During those years I learned many invaluable lessons. I rose above paralysis and fear. I helped create a new spiritual community; I learned how to see The God Who Sees Me. But the greatest lesson of all I learned from my own children.

Noa was growing stronger with each passing year. And she faced her struggles with an optimism that took my breath away. When we were on vacation in Italy two summers earlier, Noa laughed that her disabilities sounded lusciously Italian: ataxia, hypotonia. They'd go well with a plate of lasagna and a bottle of Chianti.

What a remarkable way to approach challenges. Individual differences are exotic, beautiful in their uniqueness. In the face of every roadblock there will always be a secret meandering path to take. A path unspoiled by the careless masses. Your path. A path that opens up to unanticipated splendor.

Seven years had passed and my little girl was taller than I was. Ever since Adi and Noa were old enough to stand, we'd been measuring them up against the wall in Noa's bedroom right next to the light switch and marking off the date and their height. We painted Noa's bedroom several times over the years. It changed from a baby white to a girly bubble-gum pink to a teenage bright red. But we were always careful to tape over the measuring area. It's a long strip of white with a lot of smudged fingerprints on it and all the milestones scribbled in pencil. And now there was that notice written in caps: "NOA BEATS MOM!"

In late January I was driving in the car with Noa and she asked me if she could have a rock-climbing party for her twelfth birthday. I froze. I'd always been so careful to protect Noa from disappointment. All those years I'd gone to great lengths to create parties where she wouldn't get left out or fall behind or feel that her friends surpassed her. We'd had tea parties, manicure parties, crepe parties . . . all sedentary and sweet. I said, "No, I don't think it's a good idea." "But why?" she pressed me. "It's too expensive," I said. "Let's have a party in our backyard," I suggested. But day after day Noa kept pushing for the rock-climbing party. Eventually I gave in. But I was still worried.

On the day of the party, held at a climbing gym, Noa put on a climber's harness, and to my amazement, she pushed with her legs and pulled with her arms and boldly made her way up the wall. It wasn't easy, but she climbed and climbed. She was fearless, beaming with joy. She made it all the way up to the twenty-four-foot ceiling of the gym. And then she rappelled down and started to climb right back up again.

I was so wrong about her. Adi was right, "Inside she's strong."

During the party I looked across the gym and there was a boy about Noa's age who was too frightened to climb. His father was encouraging him, but he stood frozen in place. His muscles were strong, but his fear was stronger still.

That day my daughter taught me an invaluable lesson: Our greatest disability is fear, our greatest strength is courage.

In climbing, it's the smoothest surface that is the most treacherous. Just imagine what it would be like to scale a polished marble wall. A rough, rocky landscape is fertile ground for ascension. I told myself, *If you want to rise up, don't fear the bumps. Turn every stone into a step.*

As I looked around the gym that day, I couldn't help but wonder if the key to *my life will begin when* was embedded in that rock wall. The beckoning stones gave me my answer. The challenge in life is as simple as this: Do I stare at the wall or do I climb?

fɪfty-tHRee

Nerve succeeds!

Yiddish proverb

Watching Noa scale that wall on her birthday, I suddenly remembered words my own mentor had spoken to me when I first became a rabbi. Words that puzzled me at the time they were spoken. Now, after watching Noa climb that wall, I was finally coming to make sense of them. It had taken me twenty years to understand their true meaning.

In my final semester of rabbinical school, there was only one last class I needed to take. A course in homiletics, sermon writing. I found out that I would be studying independently with a Rabbi Solomon Franks. I'd never met Rabbi Franks, so I didn't know what to expect. On Monday when I came to Rabbi Franks's office I found a little old man who was hard of hearing. I said, "Hello, Rabbi Franks." He said, "What did you say?" I shouted, "HELLO, RABBI FRANKS. I'm Naomi Levy." He smiled and said, "Well, come in, sit down my child." I thought to myself, "How am I supposed to deliver sermons to a man who can't hear?" It seemed ridiculous, a waste of time . . . until he made me preach my first sermon. And all at once I realized his wisdom, his ability to understand even what he seemed not to hear.

I grew very attached to Rabbi Franks. Each of our meetings took me deeper into religious thought. I wrote and wrote; he evaluated and gently corrected. After a while I would leave his study and find myself in tears. At first I didn't know exactly what made me cry, then I realized that each week as I left, I worried whether Rabbi Franks would be there the next week. It was difficult, growing so close to someone who had so little time left.

I continued to worry, and Rabbi Franks continued to wander into his office each week to meet me. He had my grandfather's smell. The sharp, soft scent of a strong man turned frail. He always wore a big wrinkled raincoat even on the sunniest of days and he'd wander into his office looking a little lost and sit behind his desk, which was always covered with piles of paper and files and books and a crumpled-up brown paper lunch bag. His pants were pulled high and belted around his chest. He'd look at me from behind his thick glasses and he'd say in a voice both higher and softer than any man's I'd ever heard, "What have you brought me today?"

When the term ended and I was about to become a rabbi, I turned to Rabbi Franks and asked, "Rabbi, what words of wisdom do you have for me as I become a rabbi?" He sat for a moment in silence.

And then he spoke these words: "Never . . . wear . . . brown."

That was it. That's all I got. Never wear brown? Was he kidding? I was flabbergasted. Those were Rabbi Franks's final words of wisdom to me? Didn't he have any words of Torah for me?

I spent so many years trying to understand what "Never wear brown" meant. And now, watching Noa on that climbing wall, I was finally beginning to understand. Rabbi Franks complained that brown was a wishy-washy color. A drab color. I think he was telling me, "If you're going to be a rabbi, then be a **bold** rabbi, be a brave rabbi. Open people's eyes, challenge their minds, wake up their souls, comfort their broken hearts."

I could suddenly see that Rabbi Franks, may he rest in peace beneath God's shelter, was telling me, a frightened, insecure rabbi, a lesson that applied to all people: *Don't let fear stunt you. Live with courage, act with courage, speak with courage, teach with courage, take risks with courage, make mistakes with courage, pray with courage, fight for justice with courage, face painful times with courage, lift others up with courage, say the word "No" with courage. Say the word "Yes" with courage too. And yes, dress with courage. Be **bold**.*

Noa's twelfth birthday was a lesson in tenacity and courage. Noa was bold. She had disabilities and she was brave. She was straining upward, pushing forward. The climbing party was a preface to her next milestone. Now she was setting her sights on her Bat Mitzvah, preparing herself to step up to the pulpit with pride. Several months earlier she had fantasized about sheepishly hiding beneath her prayer shawl at her service. I was watching Noa transform before my eyes, like a bud preparing to unfold. I could see that her Bat Mitzvah was going to be a revelation. There was nothing brown or wishy-washy about Noa's determination. She was all neon.

fifty-four

A child's wisdom is also wisdom.

YIDDISH PROVERB

I‍T WAS Noa's Bat Mitzvah day. That morning I found myself reviewing all the ways I had tried to protect her from this day: *We'll just do a symbolic service. It will be an abbreviated service. She'll just read a small prayer. We'll only invite our family and closest friends. We'll do it in our backyard.* I wanted to protect Noa. I wanted her to feel safe to be herself. Noa had wanted it that way too. She wanted to learn the bare minimum and be done with all the expectations of a Bat Mitzvah.

But Noa proved me wrong and she proved herself wrong too. She studied and learned and excelled. At every turn when she was ready to call it a day, it was Adi who refused to let her back down. Every month or so Noa would turn to Adi and ask him to do the rest of the Torah readings for her at her Bat Mitzvah. I was all for this. I thought it would be nice for him to help his sister out. But Adi would say to her, "Noa, you are so fooling Mom. Stop pretending you can't learn any more. You know you can learn more." Then miraculously Noa would push herself and learn yet another section of the Torah reading.

Instead of an abbreviated service, Noa was about to chant seven sections from the Torah, the entire Haftorah—the section from the Prophets—and much of the prayer service itself. Instead of a private gathering in our backyard, she was about to take the pulpit before a community of 350.

As the service began, she boldly stepped up to the pulpit wrapped in her prayer shawl with delicate white fringes and I flashed on my little girl in her fairy wings. I whispered my father's prayer to her, "I want you to shine."

She was radiant, praying, chanting, blessing. All the fear departed from her. It was as if she was leading the service from her living room. She looked around the room, made eye contact with all those who had come to share in her joy.

When we were creating her Bat Mitzvah invitation, I had written the word "Celebrate!" on the cover. And Noa corrected me. She said, "The word 'celebrate' makes it sound like it will be just a big party." Noa offered her suggestion: "REJOICE." Yes, we had all come to rejoice and to give thanks.

Now she stood before us to deliver her sermon. Rob and I sat in the front row. Suddenly he grabbed me tight and I remembered the way he had grabbed me on that awful night and made that oath: "If we get to dodge this bullet, we will never complain again." And I remembered my oath, "As God is my witness, I will fix her."

Noa began to speak. I had already read what she'd written, I thought I knew what was coming. She looked at us straight in the eye, at all of us, and said, "Today I'm going to talk to you about a very simple topic: Is life fair? Sometimes you follow all the rules, but still things don't work out for you. My Torah portion is about trying to make an unfair world a little bit more fair."

Suddenly Noa stopped reading the script before her. I started to worry for her. She looked at us all head-on and began talking. She lifted herself above the script and started talking to us from her heart.

She said:

No matter how many rules you follow, life isn't fair, it just isn't. In my life, I have physical disabilities and learning disabilities and I don't find it fair. I always wanted to be one of those people who has it easy, but I can't because that's the way I am. But then again, Moses had disabilities and he didn't do so bad!

Sometimes you might be a really good person, but you won't be able to fulfill the part of your life that's missing. Some people want something in their lives and they deserve it so much, but they just can't seem to get it. But my Torah portion teaches that we don't need to walk away from Judaism or God. We need to help each other. It teaches us that we are the answer to the unfairness of life. God can be with us and watch over us, but it's our job to help people who don't have a fair life. They have no one else to take care of them except for us.

My Haftorah is also about life being unfair. It's talking to sad people, who can't have children, who are lonely. It's offering a pep talk to anyone who's ever felt down and low. My Haftorah tells us that if you don't have good luck, if you're missing something, you will find it, so don't lose hope in yourself . . .

I could hear people sobbing. There was laughter too. Noa was moving and inspiring. Usually a Bar or Bat Mitzvah is a time for a child to demonstrate to adults what he or she has studied. But on this day, Noa arrived to share her wisdom, to teach adults the knowledge she had gained through life experience. With a sweet smile she taught us about faith, gratitude, and perseverance. She spoke freely and brilliantly. My wobbly child stood tall and strong. She was telling us with her body, "I'm here to stay!" Noa gave everyone in that sanctuary a gift that day—a gift of light and grace.

When Noa stopped speaking I heard thunderous applause. Rob and I were sitting in the front row just holding on to each other for dear life. And then I slowly turned my head around to see something I've never seen before at any prayer service. The entire community was on its feet giving Noa a standing ovation. She stood there aglow with an expression that was a mixture of humility and pride and took in all the love coming her way.

I couldn't possibly have envisioned this day. Noa proved something to herself that day, a lesson that will last a lifetime. She lifted herself above the script. There was quite a script that had already been written for her: *She'll never live. She'll never walk. She'll never learn.* She was writing a new ending, living a new beginning.

After the service, a wonderful doctor who goes to Nashuva came up to me and said, "Naomi, I hope you won't take this the wrong way . . ." Not a great way to begin a conversation. I was cringing. Was he going to insult me or my child? He continued, "Listening to Noa, it was like hearing you . . . but better."

My heart was overflowing with pride.

The bald angel's prophecy had indeed come true, "She's going to surpass you."

afterword

Bygone troubles are good to tell.
YIDDISH PROVERB

A ND THEY all lived happily ever after?
Well . . .

There's a famous joke about a Jewish mother who is walking on
the seashore with her little boy. Suddenly a huge wave comes and
sweeps the boy out to sea. The mother gets down on her knees, looks
up to the heavens, and prays, "Bring him back to me, God, save him,
I'll do anything, I'll never complain again." Suddenly another huge
wave comes and washes the boy back to shore as good as new. The
mother hugs and kisses her son, then she looks the boy over and
shouts up to the heavens: "He had a hat!"

I can't say I have no complaints. I wish life were easier for Noa;
so does she. I wish she didn't have any obstacles to overcome, any
barriers in her path.

But Noa is an incredibly wise soul, full of so much light, and
she's getting stronger each day and learning more each day. Just yesterday a friend of mine asked Noa what she wanted to do when she

237

grew up and Noa said, "I want to help people. I don't mean I want to help kids with their art projects, I want to help people find their way. I'm good at helping people find their way." For that and for so much more, I am grateful, overjoyed.

I know I'm blessed with so much. I have an incredible husband, two amazing kids, meaningful work, true friends, the love of family, a beautiful sacred community, two dogs, three chickens, and Rob's most recent acquisitions: two goats!

I've learned quite a bit over the past seven years. I've lived as Mara and as Naomi. I've learned about fear and faith and love and perseverance and luck and friendship and family. I've learned about falling and rising and shining. I've dreamed of a heaven and found it here in luminous, ordinary days; yes, the moon is in the ocean. I've learned many lessons from the Waiting Room—that you can even find grace in the wilderness. I've learned about God and angels and prophets and patience. I've learned that this very day is the only day I've got; perfect or not, it belongs to me and my real life isn't somewhere off in the future, it's right here with the chickens and the goats.

I've learned that a good push is a great thing and that when you do just one thing, many surprising things can start happening.

I've learned about laughter and courage and dreaming and I've learned about stillness. I've learned about the power of prayer and the power of glue. I've learned I have the power to tame all sorts of monsters. I've learned to worry less about catching up and more about opening up. I've learned about the beauty of community, the strength of many voices joined together in prayer, and the inspiration of turning prayer into action. I've learned to lean on people, to look for openings before I run headfirst into a wall. I've learned that time isn't on anyone's side.

Sometimes I wear brown, sometimes I have fears, sometimes I forget that the moon is always full even when it's hidden.

It's been seven years since Dr. Becket called and we still don't have a name for what Noa has. All her doctors agree that it isn't fatal or degenerative, but her condition is still a mystery, still a fog.

Last week Toba and I studied this verse from the Book of Exodus together: "And Moses approached the fog where God was." I thought to myself, a life with God doesn't mean a life of clarity. Life is uncertain, life is unfair, life is chaotic, and God is in the fog. We don't have to search for holiness anywhere else but in the imperfect, hectic world we live in.

We all get blindsided by life, we all get stuck, we all imagine that the right life or the right answer is somewhere off in the distance, but the real life we've been searching for is here in the fog.

So, as this book comes to a close I leave you with three thoughts. I hope you will put them on your heart, I hope they will seep in when you need them the most:

I want you to shine. Inside you're strong. And . . . Hope will find you.

Hope will find you. That's a pretty bold promise.

It's not something I believed. I thought it was our job to find hope or to hold on to hope. Because if you lose hope, how will you ever get it back again?

But Noa taught me to see that hope was looking for me, that hope would track us all down.

It's even okay to lose hope sometimes, not the end of the world, because hope won't lose you. Hope's got your number and your address. It's personal.

But it's not passive. Hope, I've learned, is about stepping inside life instead of waiting on the sidelines. It's about welcoming what's there. Because when you open yourself to it, hope is everywhere.

Hope will find you. Yes. A pretty bold promise.

I'm no longer one of the skeptics.

Once I started believing it, I started seeing it. Hope comes in the form of helping hands. It comes when someone offers the words you need to hear just at the moment when you need to hear them most. Hope arrives in all sorts of disguises.

When hope comes, offer it a chair.

acknowledgments

I am grateful for the unwavering support of my agent, Esther Newberg, a true advocate and adviser. Thanks to my editor, Trace Murphy, who offered me his sage counsel and guidance. Thanks as well to Kari Stuart.

I owe a deep debt of gratitude to my friends Jack Behr, Carol Taubman, Rabbi Stewart Vogel, and Rabbi Toba August, who all generously read multiple versions of this manuscript and graced me with their wisdom. Ed Solomon patiently taught me the right questions to ask. Dan Adler read this work with the passion he devotes to all things and with a precision that was indispensable.

Shari Edelstein and Dr. Bill Takeshita are inspirations to me; I thank them and all those who appear in the book under assumed names for generously allowing me to share their remarkable journeys.

The following friends and colleagues read this manuscript and left their invaluable imprint upon it: Rabbi Moshe Re'em, Rabbi Burton Visotzky, Rabbi Eli Herscher, Rabbi Nancy Flam, Jonathan Kirsch, Susan Freudenheim, Howard Blume, Teresa Strasser, Danielle Berrin, Rebecca Ritter, Martina Bronner, Veronica Lemcoff, Dr. Ginger Clark, and Cathy Coleman. My gratitude to Reverend Kirsten Linford, who opened a door for me, offered me her house of God, her wisdom on this book, and her lasting friendship. And thanks to all my Chevreh at IJS and RTI for their support, and to David Suissa for brainstorming titles and covers with me.

I received many blessings from my spiritual community, Nashuva, and its leaders. With you Judaism has come alive; we've created something remarkable out of nothing.

Special thanks to Brett and Rachel Barenholtz, Dr. Helene Rosenzweig and Dr. Richard Bock, Carin and Mark Sage, Andrea Kay, Jon and Julie Drucker, Norma Manrique, Dina Shulman, Avi and Wanda Peretz, Dr. Bill and Michelle Aronson, Holly and Harry Wiland, Andy and Kate Lipkis, and Roni Blau. And thanks to the members of the Nashuva band for filling my life with beautiful soulful songs to God: Jared Stein, Justin Stein, Ed Lemus, Bernadette Lingle, Fino Roverato, Jamie Papish, Alula Tzaddik, Andrea Kay, and Avi Sills.

Tragically, Rebecca Smith died in 2006 at the age of twenty-seven from complications of leukemia caused by A-T. Her father, George, died in 2005. May their memories be for a blessing, may their courage and dedication to finding a cure for A-T through the A-T Medical Research Foundation be sources of inspiration to their family and to all those whose lives they touched.

I am blessed with the love, strength, and guidance of my mother, Ruth Levy, Bubby extraordinaire; her wisdom sustains me. Today is the Yahrzeit of my father, George Levy, of blessed memory, the anniversary of his death. His love and wisdom continue to shine upon me and light up my days. I thank my siblings, whom I can always count on: Dr. Miriam Levy, Dr. Daniel Levy, and David Levy. And I thank all my brothers and sisters-in-law and all my nieces and nephews. My in-laws, Sari and Aaron Eshman, are powerful role models and sources of inspiration, love, and support. A special thanks to my sister-in-law, Jill Eshman, who took my author photo.

My husband, Rob Eshman, is my love. He is my personal chef, my personal editor, and my personal confidant. He's read this manuscript more times than he would care to remember, and with each read he's lifted me higher. He's given me my children. And he's also given me two dogs, three chickens, and two goats. I'll never leave town again.

My children, Adi and Noa, are God's gifts to me. They are my lights, my mentors, my greatest blessings, my comfort. They both read this book and they both made it better. They make me better all the time.

Whole and complete, this work is my prayer to God, Creator of all.

18 Sivan 5770
May 31, 2010
Venice, California

about the author

NAOMI LEVY, author of the national bestseller *To Begin Again* and *Talking to God*, is the founder and leader of Nashuva, the Jewish spiritual outreach movement. Named one of the fifty top rabbis in America by *Newsweek* magazine, she was in the first class of women to enter the Conservative rabbinical seminary. Naomi has appeared on *Oprah, The Today Show*, and NPR. She lives in Venice, California, with her husband, Rob Eshman, and their children, Adi and Noa.